FRANZ SCHUBERT IN HIS TIME

ERNST HILMAR

FRANZ SCHUBERT
In His Time

Translated by
Reinhard G. Pauly

AMADEUS PRESS
Reinhard G. Pauly, General Editor
Portland, Oregon

© 1985 as
Franz Schubert in seiner Zeit
by Hermann Böhlaus Nachf. Ges.m.b.H., Vienna

Translation © 1988 by Amadeus Press
All rights reserved

ISBN 0-931340-07-1
Printed in Singapore

AMADEUS PRESS
9999 SW Wilshire
Portland, Oregon 97225

Library of Congress Cataloging-in Publication Data

Hilmar, Ernst.
  Franz Schubert In His Time

Translation of: Franz Schubert in seiner Zeit.
  Bibliography: p.
  Includes index.
  1. Schubert, Franz, 1797–1838. 2. Composers—
Austria—Biography. Schubert, Franz, 1797–1828.
I. Title.
ML410.S3H5613   1988   780'.92'4 [B]   88-10408
ISBN 0-931340-07-1

Contents

Instead of a Preface:
Schubert in "Our" Time

For many years musical scholars have diligently endeavored to shed light on the life and works of Franz Schubert. His every written utterance has been published and duly assigned its place. Great care was lavished on a new, complete edition of his works; one conceived as a "definitive" edition.[1] Schubert research was established on a solid footing: one took pride in establishing dates of composition, in locating new versions of already known works and, occasionally, of previously unknown material.[2] Schubert became caught up in a process that had started with Bruckner, and most recently Haydn, among others: the belief that one had to speak of a "new Schubert image." Musical journalism no doubt is primarily to be thanked for this.

It is natural that Schubert, like Bruckner or Haydn, should from time to time become the subject of renewed investigations, which should lead to more or less valuable publications. Generally speaking, however, such scholarly and literary activities do not lead to new appraisals of a composer's work. Today's and yesterday's Schubert fans proceeded from a wide variety of points of view and arrived at equally divergent conclusions.

Music historians, specifically Schubert specialists, have to date been unable to present to the musical public a picture of Schubert as a musical personality—as one who has become "legendary" in the best sense of the word, like Beethoven. The sentimental picture of Schubert as "Schwammerl,"[3] as a member of a comfortable, middle-class, *Biedermeier** environment can be traced back to an unfortunate novel that should never have been written. It is a picture all too firmly established. Solid musical scholarship has been unable to replace this popular image. In short: today's image of Schubert is not a new but the old, only too well known one. Even those who claim to love and understand music are reluctant to abandon it.

Generations of music lovers have gladly written about Schubert, but from today's vantage point we are uncomfortable with the results, with the lovingly exaggerated accounts. Schubert is remarkable in the way in which he manages to elude his biographers. Few critical events seem to have shaped his life, but it may have been eventful enough to suit him. Quite likely he preferred writing music to supplying literary documents for the delectation of posterity. When looked at in this way we may gladly put up with the small amount of documentation—small when compared with his musical legacy.

In spite of the publication of annotated *Documents*[4] and *Recollections*[5] much of his character remains obscure. As a result, curious and questionable legends have arisen. If a disturbingly large volume of Schubert literature which puts him on a pedestal but paints a shallow, trivial picture has been published, the indefatigable "Schubertians," his friends near and far, must be held responsible. Decades after his death a number of his friends, upon invitation, suddenly "remembered" things, hoping, no doubt, to add to their own prestige by having been associated with the composer. Thus their accounts may make pleasant reading but cannot be taken seriously.

*For further discussion of this term, see, among others, Alice M. Hanson, *Musical Life in Biedermeier Vienna*, (Cambridge, 1985) p. 1f.

The same is true of the few pictures of Schubert and his immediate circle of acquaintances. The "pictorial tales" by his friend Moritz von Schwind, created after Schubert's death, are well known and loved. The painter, in true romantic fashion, presents us with an idealized image far removed from reality. Only his imagination, hardly affected by a sense of historical accuracy, could have inspired these scenes, playful and serene, of sociable evenings in the circle of Schubert's friends.

Thus we know very little today of Schubert—his education, his interest in events of the day, his opinions, positive or negative, of his fellow composers. We are in the dark about his knowledge of literature and his intentions for the interpretation of his music.

His biographers generally viewed him as a *Biedermeier* man, extremely good-natured—as one who loved sociability and liked his friends to pay the bills.

It may be that some Schubert lovers, on examination of the popular, stereotyped image, felt slightly uncomfortable with it. It just doesn't fit most of his music to which history, long since and without reservation, has affixed the label "masterworks."

Schubert's allegedly facile manner of composing is pure invention, together with many other tales about him. No other composer has the distinction of having been the subject of so many sentimental accounts. By 1928 more than fifty novels with Schubert as the central figure had been written; in that centennial year the number was doubled. There was no lack of pot boilers, for the hope that writing about the "sadness of his soul" would result in specially good sales was inextinguishable. The concept of Schubert the minstrel (*Spielmann*) also proved popular as revealed by many of the Schubert fiction titles.

To write about Schubert today requires dealing with fragments, so a factual biography would amount to a stringing together of documents with connecting commentary. For this purpose the *Documents of His Life,* mentioned above, are preferable. Another scholarly undertaking, probably difficult to read, would be an analysis of his music. Even such a project would not be basically new; it also might fail to satisfy a fairly large group of readers who consider Schubert's oeuvre to be "generally familiar." To refute that claim might be the subject of a special study. Of his nearly 1000 compositions[6] only a modest number has become part of the general concert repertory, and the response to the published catalog of his complete works has not been overwhelming. In this Schubert and other composers suffer from the attitude of the general public which tends to avoid the "new", i.e., the unfamiliar—even if the "new" comes from the past.

What, then, does today's reader expect from a book about Schubert? It has become fashionable to go beyond monograph and analysis: to deal with the composer and his time, to include everything from political events to fashions in clothing. The trend has grown to a minor industry reflected in the published catalogs of exhibitions about great composers and their times. Catalogs of this kind have grown far beyond the basic purpose of providing helpful information for the visitor; some have become large volumes, multifaceted compilations.

A book entitled *Schubert In His Time,* rather than *Schubert and His Time,* need not claim to be a comprehensive cultural history. It need offer vignettes only, and even these may not supply much factual material that is new to the historian and Schubert expert. What is new is the attempt to provide a different perspective on what has been previously known. If some of our observations appear to be critical of earlier writing about Schubert, perhaps this will stimulate the reader not to accept as "irrevocable" everything sanctioned by tradition. To look

10

at the sources need not lead to the expected conclusions: every document allows different interpretations. And in doubtful cases let the reader once more turn to the *Documents.*

Schubert's Years of Apprenticeship: Political and Other Aspects

During Schubert's childhood, in which music quickly assumed an important place, the political upheavals of the age affected him only marginally. The unstable conditions must have affected his parents' financial condition, but they had been forced to struggle all along, their horizons limited by concerns for their day-to-day existence. The continuing Napoleonic threat to Austria had little effect on their modest standard of living.

This political uncertainty understandably fanned some flames of patriotic feeling among the Schuberts. Franz Theodor Schubert did not fail to confess publicly his loyalty to the Imperial family. When, in June 1814 after the Paris peace treaty, Emperor Francis I returned to Vienna, the Schubert residence, Säulengasse 10, Himmelpfortgrund, was among those distinguished by festive illumination, together with a banner proclaiming loyalty to "The Best of Emperors."[1] Patriotism of this kind has nothing to do with political convictions and is insufficient evidence for the conclusion that politics was a subject of conversation in the Schubert household. Nor should we attribute too much importance to the matter: undoubtedly questions about schooling and, especially, music were the principal concerns.

Later in life Schubert's brother Ferdinand, three years older than Franz, drafted an autobiography[2] in which, significantly, he treats no subjects other than school and music. One gains the impression that the political events of the day, treated by others in great detail and greatly affecting society, had no influence on his personal growth. In this Ferdinand represents the typical government official, immune to temptation and concerned only with his career as a teacher-musician. In some ways Ferdinand had charge of his younger brother, but it would be a mistake to hold him responsible for Schubert's purported lack of touch with the real world. There are no proofs for such a contention; moreover, once Schubert entered the *Stadtkonvikt* he displayed a quite different orientation. Actually there is little to be gained by making assertions of any significance about his earlier life. One can prepare comparative chronological tables (as we have done in the Appendix of this book), but for the earliest years these juxtapositions provide few meaningful insights into musical matters. It may be interesting to learn that Haydn's famous *Emperor Hymn* was heard for the first time in the year of Schubert's birth, or that Beethoven's First Symphony was performed in Vienna, at a concert in the Burgtheater, when Schubert was four—but we cannot read any meaning into such facts.

Rather it is worth mentioning that Schubert's musical talent flourished, uninhibited by his rather drab domestic surroundings. His father, Franz Theodor, has often been described as a teacher *par excellence* and a strict authoritarian, but he also knew how to advance his son's talent by taking the right steps at the right time. Thus he approached the teacher of composition, who was then most respected and most influential, who was familiar, though not always successful, with all the current musical trends, and who had the right connections both in society and the government bureaucracy. This was Anton Salieri who had come from Venice and who by then had held for some time a number of important posts. There was no doubt about his artistic horizons. Schubert was introduced to Salieri some time before his official entrance examination and admission as choir boy to the Court Chapel, a fact heretofore unknown to Schubert scholars.[3] Some kind of private instruction may also have been involved.

So it seems reasonable to conclude that Schubert's course of study was decisively influenced by Salieri. There is also the further possibility that Salieri recommended and prepared the way for his admission to the *Stadtkonvikt* in the fall of 1808.

The *Stadtkonvikt* was located near the Old University and was associated with the Academic *Gymnasium*. It had an excellent academic reputation and assured its pupils (none of them of the nobility but rather from the educated middle class) of an outstanding education. It is to be noted that Franz was the one member of the Schubert family who was accorded this preferential education—a situation which suggests that other influential supporters had a hand in his enrollment. Salieri certainly does not appear to be the unprincipled intriguer, jealous of the success of others, as Mozart lovers are wont to depict him. Schubert may well have viewed him as a benefactor and a teacher who gave him excellent grades—viewed him as Rochlitz did who considered him

> a most charming human being, friendly and glad to be of service, benevolent, enjoying life, given to wit and endless anecdotes and quotations. A delicate, attractive little man with fiery eyes, dark skin, always clean and attractive, with a lively temperament, quick to lose his temper but easily reconciled.[4]

Salieri was the first person of distinction whom Schubert met and furthermore one from whom he garnered ideas to be used in his own composing. And compose he did, at the age of 12 if not before!

15

The *Konvikt* was under the administration of the strict Piarist fathers. While there, Schubert continued to discover means to develop his musical gifts. Not that life in the school was a bed of roses. The very select body of students—Vienna then had about 200,000 inhabitants— was expected to demonstrate unusual diligence. Passing grades were required in Latin and mathematics; later also in Greek. Failure to maintain grades in any subject resulted in dismissal. No visits to the parental home were allowed except during vacations. The result of this was to loosen family ties. Music was an important subject of study due not only to the prescribed curriculum, but also to the interests of many of the students matriculated. According to guidelines issued by Emperor Francis I music was to be

> a means to develop esthetic sensibilities, one of the noblest and most innocent entertainments but also, for at least a large number of students, a subject for major study.[5]

Schubert quickly learned how to make the most of the opportunities available. Having left a home environment where music making had been a matter of course he now became acquainted with works for larger musical forces. His knowledge of the repertory grew by leaps and bounds. Works by Mozart and Haydn, and by many lesser masters including Leopold Kozeluch and Franz Krommer, were rehearsed and occasionally conducted by Schubert. He was fascinated by this new, immensely stimulating atmosphere and it inspired his own writing. Few of these compositional efforts from his years at the *Konvikt* have been preserved, but those few show great variety. Above all there were instrumental works including four-hand piano music, string quartets, music for wind ensemble and for full orchestra. His first attempts at music drama and the first songs also stem from these early years. Inspiration did not always come from outside sources; contacts with the musical world beyond the *Konvikt* certainly were limited and attendance at concerts or opera performances were rare events. Reports about such events, by his friends and fellow students, are unfortunately very incomplete. If the *Reminiscences* are to be trusted, Schubert attended performances of stage works by, among others, Spontini (*La Vestale*), Cherubini (*Médée*), Joseph Weigl (*Die Schweizerfamilie; Das Waisenhaus*), Nicolas Isouard (*Cendrillon*), and Gluck (*Iphigénie en Tauride*). For intensive study of works in vogue at the time he had to turn to scores, to the extent that they were available to him.

During his years at the *Konvikt,* fellow students seem to have awakened Schubert's interest in current political affairs. Though he never made grandiose statements as others did, he was, contrary to general opinion, not entirely unaffected by the happenings of the time, especially the last phase of Austria's encounters with Napoleon.

There were numerous opportunities in the Vienna of the time to compose works for special occasions. They all tended to serve the same purposes: to honor someone, issue a patriotic "call to arms," and to see one's name mentioned in public as well. Thus in 1806 Ignaz Seyfried greeted the Emperor's return after the unfortunate Peace of Pressburg by composing the cantata *The Return of the Father,* thereby furnishing public proof of his patriotism. His cantata *Austria's Day of Rejoicing* (*Österreichs Jubeltag*) on the occasion of the peace treaty with Bavaria followed soon after.[6]

In 1809 the *Landwehr* (home guard) left Vienna to engage the French armies. The steady stream of patriotic concerts and choruses did not run dry until the French occupied Vienna. During the Wars of Liberation the writers of texts and music were even busier; even Beethoven saw fit to participate in these patriotic demonstrations celebrating Wellington's victory (June, 1813) by composing *The Battle of Vittoria*. At the time the performance was a great success, one possible reason being the participation of many prominent musicians, but in the long run it rather harmed him as an artist.

The liberation from the French threat and the entrance of the Allies into Paris stimulated Schubert as well. He, too, expressed patriotic sentiments in works which, happily, never found their way into the concert halls. One of these is entitled *Auf den Sieg der Deutschen* (To the German Victory, D. 81); it includes the lines "Therefore rejoice, ye Germans, for the cursed whip at last no longer afflicts us." (Drum jubelt hoch, ihr Deutschen, denn die verruchte Peitsche hat endlich ausgeknallt.) We do not know who penned these literary gems, nor is anything known of the "poet" responsible for another composition, *Die Befreier Europas in Paris* (*Europe's Liberators in Paris*, D. 104). Schubert went so far as to make two drafts, remarkable in view of the brevity of the text which reads, in its entirety: "They are in Paris! The heroes, the liberators of Europe! Austria's father, ruler of the House of Reuss, who has rekindled their courage! Good fortune was with them: they are in Paris! Our peace now is sure." (Sie sind in Paris! Die Helden, Europa's Befreier! Der Vater von Österreich, der Herrscher der Reussen, der Wiedererwecker der tapferen Reussen! Das Glück ihrer Völker, es war ihnen theuer, sie sind in Paris! Nun ist uns der Friede gewiss.) Such a demonstrative outpouring is highly unusual for Schubert who, as a rule, chose more subtle avenues of expression. In this he differed from other major figures of the time including Beethoven, but also Carl Maria von Weber (*Kampf und Sieg*) and Ludwig Spohr (*Die Befreiung Deutschlands*) whose contributions were popular successes.

The great emotional response to events of the time found expression in Schubert's music in subtle ways. His

18

Franz Schuberts Begräbnisfeier (Franz Schubert's Funeral Service, D.79) belongs here, contrary to the opinion of the experts. Its original title was *Todesmusik* (literally "Death Music"). Schubert drafted the work in September 1813, shortly after news of the death of Theodor Körner had reached Vienna. Körner had fallen in the battle of Gadebusch, 26 August 1813. How deeply Schubert was affected appears from the work's later title, referring to Schubert's own funeral. Körner had been the Vienna *Burgtheater* theater poet from 1811 to 1813. Schubert was introduced to him by Count von Spaun; the poet and the composer became friends. According to Spaun's reliable testimony Körner was the one who persuaded Schubert to devote himself entirely to music. Körner's poetry had just been published by his father; it would seem to be no mere coincidence that Schubert would turn to composing Körner's texts at this time. This was the period of the Congress of Vienna, exciting for the Viennese whose city seemed so attractive to the mighty war lords, though the Austrian Emperor footed the bills. To those celebrating their personal role in achieving liberty Schubert seems to say: the war also had its victims. It seems to be no mere happenstance that Schubert chose Körner's martial texts such as *Trinklied vor der Schlacht* (Drinking Song Before Battle), *Schwertlied* (Sabre Song), and *Gebet während der Schlacht* (Prayer During Battle).

Schubert's song for bass solo and orchestra *Wer ist gross?* (Who Is Great?, D. 110) is his strongest commitment to Austria and her Emperor. Its text, certainly of no great literary value, may also have been written by him:

Wer is wohl gross?
Der eine Welt im Kopf trägt,
in der kein Herz dem Träger schlägt?
Der stümisch von dem Throne schaut,

den Mord und Herrschsucht ihm erbaut?
Ist der wohl gross?
Der ihn erbaut?
Wer ist gross?

Der für das Heil der Menschheit lebt,
ein Feind des Kriegs
nach Frieden strebt,
dem, wenn man ihn zum Kriege zwingt,
sich jeder gern zum Opfer bringt,
ja der ist gross.

(Who is great? He who is set to conquer the world—a world in which there is no love for him? Who fiercely gazes from a throne that is built on arrogance and bloodshed? Or he who lives for the well-being of mankind, who is an enemy of war and strives for peace? If war is forced on him, everyone gladly will make sacrifices for him, even give his life for him. Yes, he is truly great.)

It was written soon after the Emperor's return from Paris, before the Congress of Vienna. There are other poems, especially by Schiller, which, to the composer, may have seemed appropriate for the times. *Vorüber die stöhnende Klage* (The Time of Mourning is Over, D. 53), a trio for two tenors and bass; the canon *Unendliche Freude durchwallet das Herz* (Unending Joy Engulfs our Hearts, D. 54), both written in April 1813, and finally Schiller's ode *An die Freude* (Ode to Joy, D. 189) can be seen as works occasioned by events of the times.

Schubert's patriotism was not generally evident to others at this time. The 17-year-old was unknown as a composer; moreover, in times of such grave political events others much better situated assumed the position of musical chroniclers. They were largely composers of very modest talents to whom fell the glorification of the political machinations. At any rate it may surprise some to know that Schubert did not live in a world of his own, far removed from political reality as is often purported. After 1815 his patriotism developed into political awareness— perhaps another new slant on his development. He furnished ample proof of what Metternich would have considered the absence of political integrity when, in the spring of 1820, he was arrested in the apartment of his friend and former fellow student Johann Senn. This police action was motivated by fears that the student unrest in Germany might spread to Austria, demonstrations that had led to the assassination of Kotzebue, a poet and playwright with absolutist sympathies. Those who regularly gathered in inns (and they were favorite meeting places of Schubert's circle) were considered suspect. To be sure, no charges against Schubert could be substantiated except some derogatory statements directed against the authorities, so he was soon released.[7] Yet there is no doubt that he was sympathetic toward the group of students who opposed the authorities' claims to absolute power. We cannot determine today to what extent Schubert was involved in this dangerous affair since all documentary evidence, normally part of police records, is either missing or not being made available. Together with Franz Bruchmann and Josef Streinsberg, the Tyrolean Senn was the chief culprit. After 14 months in prison he was exiled to Innsbruck.

Strangely enough, no documents relative to the incident have come down to us from Schubert's circle of friends. It must have been a critical turning point in his personal development for it is reflected in his handwriting which underwent a notable change at this time. Some earlier characteristics are now replaced by others, and it is strange that these do not appear gradually but quite abruptly.[8] This points to a strong personal experience; it suggests that a dangerous run-in with the authorities left traces in his personality. Thereafter his behavior seemed clouded by a considerable degree of political resignation. It found expression in his settings of two poems by Senn, the only ones by that writer he was to compose. They are *Selige Welt* (Blessed World, D. 743) and *Schwanengesang* (Swan Song, D. 744, beginning with the words "Wie klag ich's aus"). Resignation is the prevailing mood in both. Senn's name is not mentioned in the first edition of these Lieder—omitted, perhaps, as a precaution by the publisher. The assumption that Schubert thus tried to distance himself from his friend is untenable; in such a case he would have had no reason to compose the texts in the first place.[9]

At the time of setting these texts Schubert proved his loyalty to the Emperor once more. *Am Geburtstag des Kaisers* (On the Emperor's Birthday, D. 748) was written for that occasion at the suggestion of Leopold von Sonnleithner who also conducted the performance on February 11, 1822. Thus Schubert could publicly demonstrate the restoration of his political integrity.

From Musical Salon to *Schubertiade*

At the time of Schubert's attained artistic maturity the age of the great salons was drawing to a close. He therefore was unable to benefit from a social institution that was characterized, supposedly, by special interest in music but also by lavish spending.

The salon was not a Viennese invention. During the Baroque period, then during the age of Rococo and *Empfindsamkeit,* it had been the popular meeting place of the aristocracy and high finance. Among the well-to-do French there were many for whom intellectual and artistic activities provided the reason (if not excuse) for other social activities and entertainments. There was certainly no shortage of wealthy aristocrats in Vienna. Ladies with artistic and other intellectual interests assisted them and thus furnished all that was necessary to succeed in society. The end justified the means: no expense was spared. Soon the salon, meeting at regular intervals and open to select persons, became the center of high-level political activity and intrigues of many kinds.

Art was useful and pleasant window-dressing for such machinations. One surrounded oneself with literary figures of some standing, occasionally assumed the role of supporting young, rising talents and entertained one's guests with performances of small plays, pantomimes or concerts. It was considered especially delightful to have a young composer present and to admire his latest works or his instrumental virtuosity. Music was the pleasant sugar coating, so to speak; though those in the know never denied its subordinate role. Its entertainment value was appreciated but only occasionally was it the focus of interest.

There were, however, artistic circles in which music was seriously cultivated and in which Ignaz Mosel, a chief government clerk, moved. He noted in 1808 that

> Here music achieves the miracle for which normally only love is given credit: it overcomes all barriers of society. Noblemen and commoners, princes and their subjects, officials and their subordinates: here they may sit at the same music stand. The harmony of music causes them to forget the differences in their stations in life.[1]

Credible as this description may be, one should not assume that those who organized these salons possessed much musical understanding. Nor is it likely that a more profound musical taste was cultivated in these circles than in the more modest ones of the middle class. The young Beethoven had access to the salons of nobility, but he established himself with compositions that were in line with the reigning taste; had he confronted those who maintained the noble salons with his late works their reaction would have quickly exposed their lack of artistic taste and understanding.

The politically oriented salon enjoyed its period of greatest splendor during the Congress of Vienna.

> The court, of course, was the center of all social activity. One can form an idea of the level of extravagance when one realizes that during its seven months' duration the Congress swallowed the sum of forty million francs. Aside from the court there were other palaces in which festive events took place. Indeed, one may say that almost every country was represented by the salon reigned over by some lady. France was represented by Countess Perigord, Prussia by Princess Thurn und Taxis, Austria by Countess Fuchs or Princess Fürsten-

berg, England by Lady Emily Castlereagh, Denmark by Countess Bernstorff, and Russia by Princess Bagration.[2]

The Congress was a carnival without equal. Music, dance, and theater offered a wealth of distractions. The ordinary citizens participated in two ways: they could attend the opening entertainments in the Prater (Vienna's large park, by this time open to the public) and would later pay the bills for these princely amusements through a very noticeable increase in the cost of living.

With the end of the Congress the significance of the political salon ended as well. Metternich's system of government explains this: the machinery of the state, itself corrupt, suspected revolutionary activities and intrigues everywhere. Meetings of like-minded individuals were virtually forbidden. No aristocrat of means, no member of the well-to-do middle class relished the thought of becoming the victim of informers who might infiltrate some gathering. It seemed advisable not to attract attention. Ostentatious living gave way, at least outwardly, to a modest life style. The elegant salon where one competed with the luxury of the aristocracy did not disappear altogether but, partly due to the subsequent economic depression, gradually gave way to a less pretentious, "bourgeois" salon. The latter had appeared some years before, though outclassed by those of privileged, high society. But now, at the beginning of the Biedermeier Age, these salons, better characterized as literary or cultural circles, came into their own. Best known among them was the salon of Caroline Pichler, a woman not without literary talent. She knew how to bring poets, philosophers and artists of all kinds to her home and encourage intelligent conversation. She was no match for the great "salon ladies" of her time, Rachel van Varnhagen or more notably Germaine de Staël, but her acute sense of this disparity prompted her to appraise her guests most critically. Still,

25

she was quite aware of her exalted position: after all, literary and scholarly luminaries such as Clemens von Brentano, Friedrich Schlegel, Matthäus von Collin, Grillparzer and Körner were among her guests, together with the composer Carl Maria von Weber and, perhaps occasionally, Schubert. She found words of praise for Weber and his music; but all she could say for Schubert was that he was able to express, "without trying, the beautiful and moving aspects of his compositions."[3] But music certainly was not her forte, so her pronouncements are those of one who knew how to "say something" on every subject.

In the 1820s Pichler's salon lost some of its stature. Following an impulse she once modestly referred to her get-togethers as "social evenings." But there were other art lovers among the better families who, after 1814, were still sufficiently affluent to be able to maintain some kind of salon. They included Professor Johann Zizius, Vincenz Neuling, a brewery owner, and the government councillor (*Regierungsrat*) Ferdinand Müller. There also were those who subscribed to the "musical evening entertainments" of the Society of the Friends of Music (*Gesellschaft der Musikfreunde*), founded in 1818.[4] By according music a fairly important place in their evenings they continued the tradition of former patrons who, for the most part, had been members of nobility. Unlike the latter, however, they did not commit themselves to support the artists whom they engaged. A few of these new, well-to-do patrons were high government officials, as in the case of Müller. Schubert gained access to such a music lover: Court Secretary Josef Wilhelm Witteczek, who turned out to be a particularly ardent Schubert admirer. He organized a series of "Schubertiaden" (Schubertiads) in his residence near the Court Opera. Listening to Schubert's works was not enough; he also wanted to own them. For that purpose he started a collection of copies of his friend's works.[5]

Later such social evenings with music (which existed side by side with the so-called "reading circles"[6]) were characterized as being "typically Biedermeier," which implied a considerable degree of dilettantism. There may have been musical evenings which justified this derogatory use of the term "dilettante," though there clearly also were musical gatherings of a very high artistic level. These, however, were the exceptions, not quite representative of the typical salon and devoted almost exclusively to musical performance.

The gatherings at Raphael Georg Kiesewetter's residence belong in the latter category. An official in the war ministry, Kiesewetter had since 1816 organized evenings for the cultivation of "old" music. Of similar purpose were the concerts held regularly after 1815 in the spacious quarters in the Gundelhof belonging to the lawyer Ignaz von Sonnleithner. He was proud to include among his guests well known artists such as Karoline Unger, Leopold Jansa, Karl Maria von Bocklet, Ignaz Schuppanzigh and Nestroy, whose presence guaranteed a high level of execution.[7] Then there were the orchestra practice sessions under the care of Schubert and others. These may have begun as chamber music evenings in the home of Schubert's parents. Around 1815 they had grown into a regular orchestra society under the direction of Otto Hatwig, a member of the Burgtheater orchestra. These no doubt were well above the level of dilettantism. It should be added that this orchestra society, to which Schubert belonged, was dissolved in 1820, most likely for political reasons. Again, a lack of documentation makes it impossible to prove today that this event was related to Schubert's arrest. It is entirely possible that the circle of suspects was larger than commonly assumed. Certainly some students were members of this orchestra society.

These "orchestra practice sessions" were comparable to concerts in private homes. They were thus significantly different from the Schubertiads which must be regarded as a special kind of evolution from the salons. We do not know today just how the title "Schubertiad" was chosen. The assumption that a large group gathered around Schubert in order to provide a forum lacks proof and is probably misleading. Most likely the primary objective was social. "Like-minded" people (the term itself smelled of sedition to Metternich and his infamous minister of police Sedlnitzky) simply wished to get together for social evenings. Such evenings seemed unthinkable without music, and since Schubert belonged to this circle of art lovers it was not far-fetched to come up with the name "Schubertiad." The word soon acquired such a specific connotation that it was retained after Schubert no longer took an active part and finally preferred to no longer be considered one of them.[8]

Much has been written about Schubert's circle of friends and the Schubertiads. One took turns meeting in the homes of friends or patrons who had adequate space. Many Schubert Lieder and dances were indeed heard there for the first time. The artistic level was high and particularly so, for instance, when artists of the stature of Johann Michael Vogl took part. Having retired from the Court Opera in 1821 Vogl was known as Schubert's "first interpreter of Lieder." Even among the Schubertians these evenings with Vogl were a cut above their regular gatherings, as were those arranged by Spaun, when works of chamber music by Schubert were first given.

One thinks of the Schubertiads as calm and peaceable affairs. As a consequence they conform remarkably well to the accepted stereotype of Biedermeier music-making in the home: unpretentious sociability without politics, against the politically explosive background.

Though this picture may seem overly harmless it can hardly be painted differently, due to the complete lack of documents that might even suggest the discussion of subversive ideas. One can point to Grillparzer, Bauernfeld and others who moved in this circle who never uttered an incendiary remark. Yet the very absence of testimony (and one might well review the *Documents* with this in mind) might be an eloquent silence. One cannot help wondering whether members of the circle very pointedly avoided uttering critical political remarks. Simple-minded chroniclers certainly formed part of the group. There was Franz von Hartmann from Linz who later rose to the position of president of the county court in Graz: he had nothing to hide. During his student days in Vienna Hartmann kept a diary. His comments about the Schubertiads he attended deal largely with his dancing partners with occasional references to "wonderful music." The last Schubertiad at Spaun's took place on January 28, 1828. A piano trio (probably the one in E-flat major, D. 929) was played, with the participation of truly outstanding musicians. Variations for four-hand piano also were performed. Hartmann records:

> With Enk, Louis and Jerôme I went to Spaun where Schuppanzigh, Bocklet, Linke, Schubert, and Gahy made wonderful music. The prelate of Florian was there, also the two Maiers, the Ottenwalts, Spaun's dear bride, etc; 50 persons in all . . . We danced; Frau von Ottenwalt was often my partner. Then everyone went to Bogner's where we sat until half past two.[9]

Hartmann, principally interested in a good time, often wrote about teasing and other playful doings among the Schubertians—events he considered worth mentioning.

Nor do sources make mention of arguments and only rarely of personal disagreements such as did occur even in a Schubert circle. It is a lovely picture: one gathers, listens to Schubert's music and dances. Apparently there was no critical discussion even of the music. And still, it all gives the impression of dancing on top of a volcano. Everything is "low key" and the cheerful, entertaining aspects are in the foreground. Schubert serves as the excuse to leave one's home for a social affair; the rules of what is permitted are clearly defined. One knew that such gatherings were clearly risky, so one had to take the proper precautions. After all, Metternich and his minions were suspicious of any and all gatherings.

It is very likely that their conversations included some sensitive topics. One need only consider the participants: literary people, scholars and students. It is difficult to imagine that during this period intelligent men and women, who were directly affected by the political pressures and especially by censorship, should have avoided all criticism of all this in their conversation. Hypotheses, admittedly—but the impression remains that the name "Schubertiade" may have been chosen to lend an air of harmlessness to what might have had other motives. Certainly, Schubert's music provided a welcome occasion for gathering, and undoubtedly listening to his Lieder and dances brought pleasure to all. But his role in all this isn't as clear as the Schubert literature in general would have us believe. Schubert himself, to whom this milieu supposedly meant so much, disclosed no sense of satisfaction derived from it, a fact that must seem odd to the attentive reader of the *Documents*. His letters to friends, at the time when the Schubertiads became more frequent, tell nothing of his attitude toward this kind of gathering. We only know that he avoided the "reading circles" initiated by his friend Schober, but not for lack of interest in the literature of his time. He does not seem to have been missed and his infrequent visits are hardly mentioned in the *Documents*.[10]

The Schubertiads were different: music was a key element and Schubert was a most useful performer. He even sang if no better qualified singer was present, and he accompanied or played for the dancing. At times he and a friend would launch a new four-hand composition. But he was not the central figure in all this; instead attention was focused on the entertainment itself. Only a few of the Schubertians knew how to appreciate him as a composer: Most of his works musically were beyond them. The reminiscences of his friends clearly indicate that few of them had a musically adequate education.

In all the portrait of Schubertians and Schubertiads is strangely askew: his music provided the frame and may have been the front or pretext for evening gatherings. He appears as a performer, rather silent, isolated, and hardly understood as a composer. There is a clear contradiction between this portrait and that idealized in one of Schwind's paintings *A Schubert Evening At Joseph R. von Spaun's,* but our portrait likely corresponds more closely with the facts.

Schubert and the Publishers

It would seem only right that composers should be able to count on understanding publishers, and that publishers need capable composers. Too often, though, it does not seem to work both ways. Schubert's experience with publishers was much like that of great composers before and after him: the scales were tilted in favor of the publisher.

By the time Schubert had become known in Vienna music publishing in the city had already had an artistically impressive if not long history.[1] Save for a few predecessors who really were art dealers selling some music on the side, Artaria & Co. was the first music publisher. Following several earlier and abortive attempts they founded their Viennese firm in 1770. Six years later they expanded their activities to include music selling, and in 1778 issued their first engraved music. Ignaz Pleyel, Leopold Kozeluch and Johann Baptist Wanhal were among their authors; Haydn, Mozart and Beethoven soon joined them. The firm soon became a notable competitive enterprise in the European publishing world; this in spite of many problems and complaints resulting from the poor quality of and errors in their publications. For some years Artaria had a corner on the market in Vienna.

Schubert established a contact with the firm only during his last years—an agreeable relationship, since by then he no longer was unknown. But by then Artaria had long lost its leading position. Competitors, working more efficiently and by means fair or foul, were coming to dominate the market, some of whom had learned the trade working for Artaria.

Artaria & Co., let it be said to their credit, were the first to give preferential treatment to Viennese composers. To their embarrassment they found that their high goal of publishing only the best remained unattainable. There was always a market for dance music and for arrangements, but finding buyers for works by Mozart or Haydn was not that easy. Composers had to resort to inviting the public to subscribe by publishing a notice in the official *Wiener Zeitung*—but even this did not insure good sales.[2] Nevertheless, around the turn of the century music publishing in Vienna saw an unexpected turn for the better. Prices for printed music came down in order to compete with the low rates charged by professional copyists. This trend was aided by the new process of lithography, brought from Munich to Vienna by Senefelder, its inventor. Thus the way was cleared for music on a commercial scale. S. A. Steiner, owner of the *Chemische Druckerey*, was most active in using this new printing technology, rising quickly to become one of the most important music publishers. His poor reputation did not seem to inhibit his eagerness for expansion: it was said that he was more interested in quantity than quality.

Production reached such vast dimensions that one wonders whether the competing publishers tried to create a market where there was none. Anything that was playable was offered for sale. They even ventured to issue "complete editions," assuming a demand on the part of serious musicians. It seemed to be the right time for publishing Mozart's complete works for piano, as well as those of Scarlatti and Muzio Clementi. Even Beethoven found himself in the privileged position of seeing a "complete"

34

edition of his works. Understandably, publishers were most anxious to cater to those who liked arrangements for whatever purpose. There were no legal restrictions on reprinting or arranging works, for copyright did not exist; the first steps in that direction were taken around 1818. Popular pieces were soon published in continuations or series. For this purpose Joseph Eder invented his *L'Ape musicale per chitarra,* Johann Cappi his *Musikalisches Wochenblatt,* and Steiner the series *Journal für Quartetten-Liebhaber* and *Journal pour les Amateurs de la Guitarre.* Steiner was quick to justify his undertaking: there was a "complete lack of such projects . . . one has found that not all amateurs are well served by long, difficult quartets."[3] When another publisher offered "a selection of the best pieces from older and recent operas, ballets and works of chamber music, all well arranged," one could note with satisfaction that now every music lover could have a share in the most important large works of the time.

Publishers, then as now, were not willing to take risks without some safeguards. The latter first of all required that the composer's name be well known to the public. Famous composers, of which Johann Nepomuk Hummel was one, were definitely preferred. But when it came to "serious" music even the big name did not always suffice. It therefore comes as no surprise that publishers for some years showed no interest in Schubert. There is a legend that as early as 1816 Schubert tried in vain to interest Artaria in some of his string quartets. If there is any truth to it, one can understand the publisher's negative attitude. Nor did publishers beat a path to the door of the young Beethoven, and the first publications of works by the eight-year-old Mozart were the direct result of the sensation caused by a child composer.

An additional obstacle for Schubert was his inability to gain popularity as a virtuoso performer. He was "just a composer," one of many, even if the talent of most was restricted to catering to the taste of amateurs. Even as a writer of Lieder Schubert long failed to succeed. Publishers took a dim view of any songs that went beyond those having many verses based on the same rather feeble melodic idea. Even Goethe had difficulties with the "through-composed" Lied which is evident by his failure to respond to some Schubert friends who presented the poet with Schubert's Goethe songs. Understandably, Viennese publishers had similar difficulties warming up to Schubert's Lieder: all their efforts went into selling arrangements of arias from popular operas or easy chamber music. One might respond that some of Vienna's publishers were composers themselves—but fortunately most of their creative efforts are forgotten today.

Schubert's friends were convinced that a composer didn't count until his name, better yet his music, had reached print. The first step to reach this goal was the "music supplement." Indeed some Schubert songs first appeared as supplements to almanacs, in 1818 and in 1820 (Leipzig). Such almanacs (*Taschenbücher*) appealed to the educated middle class.[5] But pointing to publication in works of this kind, popular as they were, was not enough to win over a music publisher. Other ways had to be found to help the composer on the road to success. The more renowned a publishing firm and the more powerful its owner, the less interest he showed. The fact that some publishers were of Italian origin meant nothing; they had no more artistic understanding than others and were chiefly interested in doing away with the competition. Once a publisher had been ruined another bought his firm. Cappi & Diabelli were experts at this game. At the urging of Schubert's friends they finally agreed to give him a chance, on a commission basis—an agreement that excluded any risk for the publisher.

It appears that Schubert took little interest in the first publications of his songs for which friends, on the initiative of Leopold von Sonnleithner, had advanced the money. Ignaz von Sonnleithner, father of Leopold, had the *Erlkönig,* D. 328, performed in his salon and announced its impending publication. He also sought out a suitable person to whom it might be dedicated. This was a somewhat irregular way of proceeding; as a rule the composer or publisher took care of this. But in this instance no publisher was involved, and Schubert still was so little known that he lacked the boldness to ask a person of distinction without a recommendation. Such a dedication was likely to influence sales favorably; it also normally entailed a generous gift from the dedicatee.

And so the task became Sonnleithner's. He turned to Count Moritz von Dietrichstein, a nobleman whom Schubert came to know during his years at the *Konvikt.* The letter is worth quoting, especially since it is not found in the *Documents:*

> Most noble *Reichsgraf!* I take the liberty of recommending to Your Grace the bearer of this letter, the talented composer Franz Schubert. He deserves your kindness in every way, already having charmed a knowledgeable public with several excellent Lieder. He requests Your Grace's permission to dedicate a small work to you. Wishing to publish it he hopes that by including your so very justly honored name it will have wider appeal. I feel sure that Your Grace does not need my endorsement to encourage one of our fatherland's talents, for your past encouragement and support of true artists is well known. May I take this opportunity to express to Your Highness my greatest admiration. Your obedient servant Ig. Sonnleithner.[6]

Sonnleithner also arranged for the dedication of *Gretchen am Spinnrade,* D. 118, to Count Moritz von Fries who expressed his thanks to Schubert with a gift of twenty ducats—a considerable sum at the time.[7]

Cappi & Diabelli issued the first collection of Lieder on a commission basis but saw fit not to acknowledge the nature of this arrangement when announcing the works in the *Wiener Zeitung,* instead claiming them as their own publications. They also knew how to present themselves to the public as the discoverers of a "genius." The third volume of Lieder (*Der Wanderer,* D. 489, *Morgenlied,* D. 685 and *Wanderers Nachtlied,* D. 224) was published only a few weeks after *Erlkönig.* At this time they announced that

> due to frequent requests addressed to the publishers they were prompted to present these two volumes [i.e., Op. 3 and 4] to the lovers of German song. The poetic soul of the composer is already evident in his choice of texts, but his musical understanding and setting of these poetic masterworks demonstrates the young artist's genius.[8]

Thus his first publishers eagerly called attention to their own artistic understanding, but their business dealings with the composer were another matter. Cappi & Diabelli, in spite of the commission arrangements, tried to take advantage of Schubert's lack of experience in these matters. Schubert, his self-confidence increased by the sudden public recognition, now objected more energetically to this treatment. A parting of ways was the inevitable result. The association had barely lasted two years; during this time works with opus numbers 1–18 had been published. A reconciliation with Diabelli did not come to pass until 1827. In 1824, Diabelli had become the owner of the renamed firm "Anton Diabelli & Co." which became the most influential Viennese music publisher other than Haslinger. Music history has bestowed on Diabelli the title "Schubert's chief publisher;" he seems to have grown especially fond of Schubert's works after his death. He accorded one special distinction to the Lieder he published: he neatly listed them in a thematic catalog, arranged according to the authors of the texts, giving title and incipit as well as the number of plates used. This catalog is now in a private collection and unfortunately not generally accessible.

Following the unfortunate experience with Cappi and Diabelli, Schubert did not fare much better with other publishers. Generally speaking the 1820s saw a stagnation of classical music sales. To his friend Franz von Schober, Schubert complained that "nobody bought anything, neither my works nor others—only the miserable stuff that's fashionable."[9] But things were no better elsewhere. In 1822 Josef Hüttenbrenner undertook to help his friend Schubert by establishing a connection with the Leipzig publisher C. F. Peters. He pointed out that in a good year 300 copies of one work by Schubert had been sold, but Peters' reply contained nothing but excuses.[10] First of all, he "never published anything inferior"—but he had to admit that this policy, too, was unrealistic, for "if we only sell serious music we would supply a very small public." Nor did he want to consider "new music;" he preferred to leave the risk involved to others. Of course, he considered his attitude to be good business sense. After all, it is the dream of every publisher to issue contracts for outstanding works by composers who are widely known. As Peters put it,

> once a new composer has made a name for himself and his works have received a favorable reception, then I am his man; then publishing his music fits my policy which is based on distinction rather than financial gain.

Schubert might have been consoled had he known that Beethoven was similarly treated by Peters at about the same time: he was "insufficiently known" and was forced to remain content with rejection letters full of elaborate excuses.

Schubert thus had to look further. He established contact with the Viennese Sauer and his partner

Leidesdorf. Both were musicians; one a kind of musical expert, the other a composer and arranger. But both lacked the nature suited to this line of work; not surprisingly the business (later run by Leidesdorf alone) succumbed to Diabelli's eagerness to expand. Schubert called Leidesdorf "a good person, of some depth but of a highly melancholic disposition. I'm afraid too much of it rubbed off on me. Thus neither one of us is doing well and we never have any money."[11] Sauer & Leidesdorf published 15 Schubert works, among them the *Schöne Müllerin* song cycle, D. 795. One wonders whether they really were aware of the significance of the works they published. At any rate, there seems to be no explanation for the way they treated Schubert's manuscripts. It was not the custom of the day, as other examples show, to publish a work and then discard the composer's autograph. Sauer & Leidesdorf showed unparalleled neglect in these matters: the autographs of the Schubert works they published, among them the String Quartet in A Minor, D. 804, apparently were discarded as waste paper.

In general, the publisher did not display good business sense. Following the practices of competitors he tried to take advantage of seasonal business, but sales seem to have been below expectations. "Seasonal" related to the Christmas and carnival seasons. Sauer & Leidesdorf always figure in the advertisements: they published several collections of dance music and showed imagination in their choices of titles: popular dances intended for home use.

To be sure, others offered similar fare: Cappi & Diabelli, Thaddäus Weigl ("A Musical Offering for the New Year"), Cappi & Co. ("Dance Music for the Carneval of 1825"), Pietro Mechetti ("Terpsichore") and Tobias Haslinger ("New Carneval Offerings")—they all sought their share of profit from the Viennese craze for dancing.

Schubert was well represented in such dance collections. They must have contributed to his popularity if only in a limited way.

Sauer & Leidesdorf, who favored Schubert over other composers of dance music, do not seem to have been greatly successful in this genre. Perhaps the printings were too small, or there was a lack of customers. These must be the reasons why their editions are so rare today, unlike those by Diabelli, Mollo, or Haslinger.

Schubert's cooperation with Sauer & Leidesdorf seemed to offer no promise for future success, so Schubert looked for other publishers. Having tried Cappi & Co., Anton Pennauer, and Mathias Artaria he entered into a relation with Tobias Haslinger. Alexander Weinmann, the authority on Viennese music publishers, has characterized him as follows:

> If one looks at a contemporary portrait of Haslinger one would imagine him to be a typical bureaucrat, perhaps a merchant or small factory owner, but never a man with the business acumen and the many talents of our Haslinger. He composed, arranged, sold, and published music; he was a friend of Beethoven and many renowned artists.[12]

To this "bureaucrat," the successor of Senefelder & Steiner, Schubert now turned. And Haslinger, who was also the publisher of Johann Strauss, Sr., thus enriched his catalog, already quite distinguished, with works that could bear comparison with any others—the *Winterreise* cycle, D. 911, among them. A few years later he offered further proof of his business acumen: he contested Diabelli's claim to Schubert's estate and was able to buy from Ferdinand Schubert the rights to *Schwanengesang,* D. 957.

In Haslinger and Diabelli, Vienna undoubtedly had major music publishers, but the general atmosphere in the publishing world seems to have been strained by unethical business practices of the owners. There were embittered law suits about rights, for the legal aspects of reprinting, making arrangements, and "pirated editions"; had not yet been clarified.[13] Schubert was hardly affected by these difficulties as his works had not yet become the favorites of publishers or public. There were a few unauthorized reprints of his early editions, unknown to his publisher. A. Cranz in Hamburg and F. S. Lischke in Berlin had published the *Erlkönig;* Bachmann in Hannover had brought out *Gretchen am Spinnrade.* What really encouraged publishers to engage in these outrageous practices were Rossini's operas—sure-fire successes for which opera lovers nearly went crazy. Everyone wanted to make a profit. If a publisher could not obtain the vocal score, he printed all kinds of arrangements of the most popular excerpts. The number of such publications reached dizzying heights; one must assume that a huge market among dilettantes existed. When Rossini's star waned, the situation changed at once. Loud complaints could be heard about the "sad state" of the music trade, and the list of publishers who were forced out of business grew ever longer.[14]

What convinced every serious composer to look for publishers outside of Austria were not these expected bankruptcies but the publishers' exclusive concern with local, dilettantish music-making of low quality. Schubert, too, decided to look elsewhere. After a fairly successful concert of his works in March, 1828 he could show foreign publishers written proof of his recognition as a composer. In 1826 he had failed to reach an agreement with Breitkopf & Härtel since they did not want to make a financial commitment. Next the names B. Schott's Sons in Mainz and Heinrich Probst in Leipzig sounded promising to a young Viennese composer, and so Schubert took the initiative. What he had not counted on were the complications of conducting affairs by mail and the lethargy of long-established publishers. Nor was the reigning taste in Leipzig or other German musical centers very different. Schubert had to learn that small, "not too difficult" pieces were preferred. That these publishers from the beginning offered only the most modest fees was another bitter pill. No agreement was reached with B. Schott's Sons, despite their claim to be acquainted with Schubert's "excellent compositions" and their expressed wish to acquire several of his works.[15] In October, 1828 Probst alone provided some satisfaction by publishing, shortly before his death, his Piano Trio in E-Flat Major, D. 929. This was followed in December by the Lieder, OP. 101. And this was the extent of interest shown by German publishers in Schubert's work for some years to come.

Concert Life in Vienna

During Schubert's lifetime musical dilettantism was close to reaching its greatest flowering. The term "dilettante" as used here does not necessarily have a purely derogatory meaning; most musicians did have some training. But just what level, as compared with today's standards, must remain conjectural. Nor is it clear where and from whom the many "artists" received their musical education. Until 1817 Vienna had no conservatory. Substantial teaching methods and materials were lacking, nor were there teachers of recognized accomplishment. There were a multitude of private teachers who, of course, called themselves "musical artists," but few inquired of their credentials. They had many students, for to sing or to play an instrument was considered a must in every self-respecting family. Occasionally well-known virtuosos would accept students, but then as now they were mostly concerned with advancing their own careers so were apt to spend more time on tours than with their pupils.

Around 1800 Vienna is said to have had about 2000 dilettantes—a considerable number. Not surprisingly these music lovers, coming from all segments of society, made repeated efforts to form an organization. They succeeded when in 1812 the *Gesellschaft der Musikfreunde* (Society of Friends of Music) was founded. It sponsored regular *Abendunterhaltungen* (Evening Entertainments) beginning in 1817—events that were to figure importantly for Schubert. Their *Concerts spirituels* saw the light of day in 1819. Both had as their stated purpose the "infusion of new strength into musical life."[1] Nineteenth-century Vienna had indeed need of an organization dedicated not to music-making in the home but rather to facilitating performances of symphonic and other major works. This shortcoming was noted in more or less official publications where many complained of such an under-developed musical life, restricted almost exclusively to performances in the home. So the *Vaterländische Blätter* of 1808 commented:

> If the state of musical culture corresponds to that of general intellectual development, then the inhabitants of this capital are to be congratulated. Here on any given evening there is hardly a family that does not derive entertainment from a string quartet or a piano sonata. But while much is done for so-called chamber music very few opportunities exist for the performance of symphonies, concertos etc. by a full orchestra.[2]

The correspondent goes on to point out that in Vienna the consumption of food and music seem to go hand in hand, which may be an obstacle to reforming the city's cultivation of music:

> The citizens of Vienna, while improving their minds and their taste, don't like to neglect the palate. At evening concerts it used to be quite customary to improve the orchestra members' strength and the audience's attention by serving refreshments. This practice may explain the scarcity of larger concerts in Vienna.

With the founding of the *Gesellschaft der Musikfreunde* music lovers moved to set things right. In order to demonstrate their intention to "advance music in all its branches" they undertook "monster concerts." But audience response was not always wildly enthusiastic. The performance of Handel's *Samson,* given on the occasion of the Congress of Vienna, serves as an example. The rather

46

stiff, formal etiquette observed at court forbade any applause. Caroline Pichler, speaking as a choir member rather than as a devotee of literature, observed that "this atmosphere had a chilling effect on the performers whose eagerness and enjoyment diminished."[4]

But the *Musikfreunde* did more than sponsor gargantuan performances, characterized as "music festivals." According to their statutes, *Gesellschaftskonzerte* (Social Concerts) were also to be presented but on a more modest scale. Contemporary symphonic music was to be heard featuring the most important composers. During the first years of the Society's existence, dilettantes in the negative sense of the term were in charge. A critical examination of the programs reveals that popular taste dominated these programs to a disturbing degree. Unfortunately the concerts were planned by an organization with a promising name, so they set a precedent and were widely imitated, not only in Vienna. The musical menu consisted of a mixture of many diverse offerings. Most likely the planners proceeded in keeping with their own musical interests and education and did not want to burden their audiences with "heavy" programs. They may also have hoped that variety would keep the listeners awake. But variety in fare also entailed variety in quality. This absence of concern for quality is all the more surprising since the concerts given by Beethoven required a degree of concentration that even today's music critics, who tire easily, would judge "unrealistic." Thus in his great "academy" (public concert) of May 7, 1824 Beethoven programmed the Overture in C Major, Op. 124, three excerpts from the *Missa Solemnis;* and the Ninth Symphony.

A few weeks earlier the *Gesellschaft* had held one of the four customary *Saisonkonzerte.* Aside from the obligatory symphony, this time by Haydn, there was a soprano aria from Fernando Paër's *Griselda,* the first move-

47

ment of Bernhard Romberg's Cello Concerto in G Major, Michele Carafa's overture to *Le solitaire,* Beethoven's *Opferlied* and Mozart's hymn *Preis dir, Gottheit, durch alle Himmel.* The concert thus exemplified two shortcomings common during the first decade of *Gesellschaft* concerts. No effort was made to do away with the reigning convention that any concert program "simply had to" include an Italian aria. Of the 36 concerts held before the spring of 1824 only seven lacked this Italian ornament. Also it seems to have been inconceivable that a concerto for soloist and orchestra might be given in its entirety. Usually only one movement was included, whether written by Beethoven, Spohr, or Romberg. This practice remained unchanged until the 1830s, reminding us of the programs of today's student recitals. Nor was there any reluctance about programming a single movement from a symphony, especially in Beethoven's case. (First movement of *Eroica,* May 3, 1818; first and second movements of the Ninth, December 16, 1827.)

The choice of programs showed no great inventiveness. A symphony usually came first, and it was apparently considered daring to go beyond Haydn, Mozart and Beethoven. Only Franz Krommer managed to achieve five performances between 1820 and 1827, and there were single performances of works by Eduard Lannoy, Romberg, Johann Hugo Worzischek and Ferdinand Ries. Schubert was able to hear at these concerts his Overture in E Minor, D. 648, and two vocal compositions, *Das Dörfchen,* D. 598 and *Geist der Liebe,* D. 747, but his symphonies were not programmed during his lifetime. Instead the *Gesellschaft* contributed to the familiar picture of Schubert as a writer of Lieder. The Lied was considered out of place in public concerts: being seen as a genre belonging in the home. But performances of vocal quartets were another matter: these belonged to the genre of choral music.

After the opening symphony the *Gesellschaft* concert programs proceeded in keeping with an established pattern. Everyone waited for the Italian aria, following which one expected part of a concerto. Either a choral work, usually of a hymnic, religious character, or an overture, which today seems particularly out of place, concluded the concert.

By comparison the *Abendunterhaltungen* presented by the *Gesellschaft* appear quite progressive in their programming.[5] The purpose of these events, which were somewhat intimate in nature but open to the public, was explained in the invitation of 1818:

> In their constant efforts to improve their musical activities the *Gesellschaft der Musikfreunde* has decided to schedule for the coming winter, in its own hall, the following events, all on Thursday nights at seven o'clock: Eight *Abend-Unterhaltungen*, four student, and four operatic concerts.[6]

This ambitious plan had to be reduced in scope. The "progressive" aspect was then explained in the succeeding paragraph:

> The committee charged with planning and directing these private musical events believes it can assure audiences of most satisfying musical experiences, all the more so since they have been successful in securing the participation of several distinguished artists some of whom so far have been heard in private circles only.

These promises were kept, at least in Schubert's case. From 1819 to 1828 he was represented by 26 compositions, programmed at 41 *Abendunterhaltungen*. The organizations did not, however, venture to include any of his instrumental works: when it came to string quartets, for instance, they preferred those by Spohr, Georges Onslow or Josef Mayseder. Special attention was paid to Schubert's Lieder. Since these evenings differed from the *Gesellschaftskonzerte*, they opened new vistas for Vienna's concert life.

Vocal quartets continued to have a place on these *Abendunterhaltungen,* with contributions by insignificant composers such as Ignaz Seipelt more or less competing with Schubert. Eventually the category of the Lied was favored. It stands to reason that Schubert played a major role in this development. Before and during his time there were so few significant contributions to the genre that they pale by comparison with his.

Schubert's Lieder were quite in demand for the *Abendunterhaltungen.* One heard the *Erlkönig* in January, 1821, soon followed by Schiller's *Sehnsucht,* D. 636. The latter song, like *Der zürnenden Diana,* D. 707 or *Der Zwerg,* D. 771, was requested for several later events. The interpreters were amateur singers with creditable voices: August Gymnich, Josef Götz, Franz Schoberlechner and Ludwig Tietze. The latter was once accompanied by Schubert himself (*Normans Gesang,* D. 846). Today's Schubert experts know their names but they were of little import for the world of music in general.

Aside from the purely private Schubertiaden, the *Abendunterhaltungen* of the *Gesellschaft der Musikfreunde* were the only forum where Schubert's work was regularly performed. True, this meant that one paid attention to only one category of his extensive oeuvre, but historically speaking it was a most important one. Other organizations which pretended to be more serious and more exclusive than the *Gesellschaft* performed no Schubert works at all. Among these were the *Concerts spirituels* that began in 1819. Their principal objective was the performance of complete symphonies by established composers. While laudable in theory, in practice the objective was reached only at the expense of quality. The original plan, surely dreamt up by dilettantes, called for performances without any rehearsals.

Such sight reading before a large audience was

bound to end in disaster. Later, and as a consequence of poor performances, the policy was relaxed somewhat and occasional rehearsals were held. Still, the concerts were appropriately dubbed "small town music" (*Winkelmusik*) by Beethoven.[7] The printed programs, the only remaining witnesses, tell us nothing about the quality of performances but are evidence of a substantial repertory. Among writers of symphonies Mozart, Haydn and Beethoven held first place. Sacred music was represented by Cherubini, Ignaz Seyfried, Georg Josef Vogler, Handel and Albrechtsberger.

While the *Concerts spirituels* were admittedly tainted by dilettantism, they did have one positive effect on Vienna's musical life. The programs made a point of referring to "classic" works, which was bound to be noticed by others. Schubert had written the *Hymnus an den heiligen Geist*, D. 948 for these concerts, but it was not performed until after his death while those of composers such as Joseph Eybler, Johann Evangelist Horzalka, Eduard Lannoy were. Perhaps they had better connections to the concerts' organizers.

Schubert therefore had to take advantage of another extremely popular institution: the *Virtuosenkonzerte* and, occasionally, the so-called *Wohltätigkeitsakademien* (Benefit Concerts) which had been popular since the turn of the century.

After 1800 the popularity of virtuosos increased substantially. This adulation developed quickly, and one can say that virtuosity and musical substance stood in an inverse relationship to each other. Beethoven was considered a virtuoso, but his impact on audiences was based less on manual dexterity than on his remarkable ability to express ideas through musical imagination. After him piano playing became increasingly brilliant but also mannered. Celebrated representatives of this kind of

51

keyboard virtuosity were Ignaz Moscheles, a child prodigy from Prague, and Johann Nepomuk Hummel, once a student of Mozart. Both prided themselves on their virtuosity and for many years put it to good use in their concerts. Potpourris, variations on some theme or other and fantasies formed the core of their programs which attracted large audiences. Some were subscription concerts such as the six "Dukatenkonzerte," announced in the spring of 1815 in which the violinist Mayseder and the guitarist Mauro Giuliani were featured.[8] Others were concerts or "academies" which the musicians arranged themselves.

Their usual repertory tended toward pleasing but shallow display pieces which in turn became the standard repertory of less accomplished "virtuosos," establishing a trend that was to dominate the music scene for more than a decade. Contemporaries noted and criticized the trend repeatedly, pointing out that such aberrations "cannot be overcome even by the laudable efforts of dedicated spirits."[9] According to Friedrich August Kanne, a musician and writer who from 1821 to 1824 edited the *Wiener Allgemeine Musikalische Zeitung,* such a state of musical "perversion" results when

> the taste of the public is confused—when one loses sight of the beauty of the whole and sees only insignificant details. This is indeed the state of music today: music itself does not matter, but we must have vocal display.[10]

The concert programs of Hummel and Moscheles and other virtuosos of varying degrees of skill—whether pianists or flutists, violinists or string bass players— differed from today's typical recitals, as other musicians frequently assisted the soloist. Programs of the *Gesellschaftskonzerte* may have been overly diverse, but what virtuosos chose for their recitals reflected no artistic criteria whatsoever. They based their selections on what happened to be available or on requests by well-meaning friends.

In the opinion of Kanne such haphazardous programming had an economic base:

> In choosing works for performance, variety and contrast are seen as the way to meet expenses or even make a profit, for there are few true connoisseurs of music. For reasons of economy music performance must ally itself with declamation or recitation, a strategy that will fill the hall with both educated and other listeners. Thus fashion comes to the rescue . . . This is how the "mixed" morning, noon and evening entertainments came into being. [10]

In his highly critical description of concert life, Kanne thought the public to lack adequate musical education, and he must have had his reasons. Still, he vigorously tried to point out to his readers (whom he trusted to be educated and interested) what was wrong:

> How can one hide one's displeasure about the most peculiar combinations of music and recited poetry? Such a concert is nothing but a *ragout melé*. For the economic reasons mentioned above composers and virtuosos are compelled to come up with rather adventurous choices—but the unpleasantness of it all is only accentuated by this mixing of music and recitation. One leaves the hall with a great profusion and confusion of impressions.

Kann's report is by no means exaggerated; it was true of virtually all virtuoso recitals but also those usually labelled "private concerts." But it seems odd that Schubert's participation in such performances should have been due largely to financial concerns. Organizers liked to program vocal quartets which like recitations appealed to only a limited segment of the audience. Schubert appeared only occasionally on these programs; too many other composers, often not even listed on the program, also wanted to be included. If one of his works did appear on the program, be it a new work or one which

53

had been successful elsewhere, personal connections may have made the difference. He was invited to appear on about three dozen programs, most of which featured the same artists, and almost all were Viennese. The violinists Alfred Jaëll, Leopold Jansa and Johann Georg Hellmesberger, the cellist Joseph Merk, and the horn player Joseph Lewy all included a Schubert vocal quartet on their programs.

Among pianists we find Karl Schunke from Magdeburg. His concert of March 25, 1821 can serve as a model for the makeup of the programs described by Kanne. A published review of this concert furnishes more information than is usually available and also includes some useful observations about piano performing practices of the time. Schunke's program, held in the *Landstädtische Saal*, began with Hummel's Piano Concerto in A Minor, following which he improvised. He concluded with Johann Peter Pixis' *Hungarian Rondo*. The reporter for the *Theaterzeitung* attended and recorded the following impressions:

> As usual, his playing today was assured and very precise. He proved that the piano holds no difficulties for him; he even surprised those who were no strangers to his playing. There is nothing one wishes more for this young artist than the development of his emotions . . .; so far he amazes only by perfect solutions of the tasks he had set for himself. Most effective was his rendition of the A Minor Concerto, even if the challenge of its difficulties was what attracted him to it. His improvisation lacked imagination and his performance of the rondo lacked color . . . He played on a Konrad Graf piano, probably an instrument with quadruple stringing: no other instrument would have stood up under such powerful, not to say violent treatment. Even pianists with a less athletic approach must find comfort in the thought that they may play with fire and abandon without worrying about breaking strings . . . For this we must thank our Viennese Graf. Except for his instru-

ments only the English ones can take such treatment . . . Three times within one and a half hours this instrument was subjected to very forceful and rough playing, but in the last measure it was as well in tune as in the first one . . . Herr Ruess' rendition of the wonderful *Erlkönig* by Schubert, our composer with such great promise, was not without merit. Still, whoever had heard this masterpiece for the first time as interpreted for the *Musikfreunde,* with great spirit and feeling, will never forget that occasion. Herr Sedlatzek played Keller's Variations for Flute with great virtuosity, lovely tone and good taste. Two charming ladies, through singing and recitation, eagerly contributed to the enjoyment of a fairly large audience. The Court Opera Orchestra, under the direction of Herr Kleschinsky, gave a fine rendition of the Overture to Vogel's *Demophon.* [11]

The "fine" playing of the opera orchestra may have been the exception that evening. Kanne mentions the players' lack of enthusiasm for rehearsals "since other important affairs either kept them away or caused them to be pressed for time."[12] Lack of time must indeed have been a problem: there were so many private concerts, musical entertainments, recitals by virtuosos and "academies" that popular performers could hardly have kept up with all their engagements.

Save in the case of Beethoven the programs of virtuoso concerts or academies were much alike. The recital given by the cellist Friedrich Wranitzky in July 1824, in the *Redouten Saal,* serves as an example. It opened with the *Fidelio* overture. The first movement of Romberg's Fifth Cello Concerto followed, played by Wranitzky whose tone "left a great deal to be desired."[13] Next came *Variations For Two Horns* by Conradin Kreutzer, after which a vocal quartet by Schubert was sung. The child prodigy Leopoldine Blahetka then played one of her own compositions on the piano. (Schubert's *Erlkönig* had been on her concert program in March 1824.) To end the program Wranitzky appeared once more playing variations by

Anton Wranitzki.

Such mixed fare also characterized the popular academies where the organizers were more interested in making a profit than presenting good music. The critics rightly complained about such incompetent programming, but they fell silent when other events attracted their attention, such as the Vienna appearance of Niccolò Paganini. But then even Schubert was fascinated by this outstanding virtuoso.

It is true that great and not so great virtuosos made a splash in Vienna, and that the city was the center of private recitals in which good and bad dilettantes competed with each other. But Vienna also was the home of such composers as Beethoven and Schubert and of performers who pursued unpopular but sound artistic goals unaffected by the fashions of the day, who left a strong imprint on the musical scene. One of these was Ignaz Schuppanzigh. He was the first to organize string quartet concerts on a subscription basis, from 1804–1816 and again after 1823. His cultivation of Beethoven's music set an example for the city. Schuppanzigh was not a virtuoso violinist, but he had a distinct musical personality that commanded respect. His programs appealed to an audience of connoisseurs, and happily there was such an audience. The critics, too, appreciated what he was doing. When in 1827 Schubert's Octet, D. 803, was first heard in one of his quartet concerts, the thoughtful review in the *Theaterzeitung* was thoroughly supportive and was marked by the careful use of the terms "art" and "artist":

> Visiting artists, connoisseurs and amateurs who attended these quartet recitals assured us that at no time or place had they encountered such perfect execution. Most of these performances could indeed be called "perfect." None of the players sought the spotlight; no single part, no single passage was allowed to dominate. How different from other such events! All four artists have

but one common goal; they pursue it with supreme command of their instruments, which is reflected in their subordination to the work as a whole. They are clearly aware of their goal, always alert. As a result these quartets are becoming models of taste and execution. They have remained in the repertory for years, with growing public interest and applause.[14]

The review is most flattering for Schuppanzigh; by implication it makes an unflattering contrast to other quartet concerts and Viennese public concerts in general. This "wanting to be noticed" seems to have characterized most musical events. If programs not only contained excessive variety but also lacked artistic integrity one can understand Kanne's dissatisfaction with the direction in which the concert life of his day was moving. He thought he knew the reason for such an absence of taste and understanding: the "lack of warm feeling for music was caused by a general falling off in matters of morality."[15]

Contrasts:
Suburban Theaters and the
Cult of Rossini

Even Schubert's contemporaries did not take his stage works very seriously, and this is still true today. Music historians have not dealt with them in any systematic way; one gains the impression that they prefer to avoid any serious attention to the matter. No writer has flatly asserted that Schubert's dramatic efforts were mistakes, or that he lacked a feeling or talent for the stage. After all, the music in the operas was written by Schubert, and no one would be so bold as to question the stature of his music in general. Thus one concludes that the problems are to be found in the texts he used. About this there seems to be general agreement: the texts are bad (even Goethe's text for *Claudine von Villa Bella*, D. 239), therefore no viable operas could result. In saying this one forgets that not all of Mozart's librettists were geniuses, and that some operas by later composers were based on all but incomprehensible stories; yet they managed to maintain themselves in the repertory. So we might conclude that there are other reasons why Schubert's operas were ill-fated.

If one turns to the routine, run-of-the-mill operas of his contemporaries, one can understand that reigning taste did not allow any experimentation with the genre. It is also safe to assume that once he had studied Gluck and Mozart, as we know he did, he was not eager to follow the Italian style. Evidently his teacher Salieri concurred in this judg-

59

ment, as is shown by Schubert's early stage works.

Further, Schubert faced a nearly impossible task. After Mozart, any serious composer undertaking to write an opera or *Singspiel* had to look for a new musical approach. Beethoven was sufficiently courageous to try it once. He did not find it an easy task; the three versions of *Fidelio* written within 10 years are eloquent testimony. Yet among the composers of the period his opera has a place distinctly its own, in view of its highly charged ethical content.

The writing down of the third version of *Fidelio* coincides almost exactly with the first version of Schubert's three-act opera *Des Teufels Lustschloss,* D. 84. The coincidence may seem strange, but it is an historical fact. Stylistically the two are worlds apart. One must seek the explanation in the search for an entirely different dramatic concept, not by dismissing Schubert's opera as a "the work of youth." Schubert was quite caught up in the reigning operatic tastes of the time, a matter to which I will return. Even his later operas demonstrate his difficulties in this preoccupation. The times hardly could have been less favorable for the development of opera. Charlatans and speculators, together with more serious devotees, have always been attracted to the theater. Whenever such interests gain the upper hand the change from good to bad theater soon follows. Loss of substance is readily accepted by a public which typically prefers shallow entertainment. Such was the state of Vienna's theaters and its enthusiastic public when Schubert undertook to come to terms with opera.

Aside from the Burgtheater and Kärntnertortheater Vienna had in the early 19th century three significant suburban theaters to which the citizens flocked in the evening, along streets that didn't lack danger. Unlike the two national theaters these suburban houses were allowed to stage works in which only German was used. Each house had its own tradition but one purpose united them: to approach as closely as possible the standards of magnificence of spectacle and variety of programming set by the national theaters.

The Theater an der Wien, built by Schikaneder in 1801, met these requirements particularly well.[1] Its stage was considered the most modern and most beautiful in Vienna, well-suited for large productions of all kinds. Schikaneder preferred plays with music—virtually ignoring spoken plays, as performances of the latter, especially the "classics," were made very difficult due to strict censorship. It took Vienna's occupation by the French to allow greater literary freedom. But even then foreign, and particularly German, playwrights dominated the repertory, with Kotzebue's dramas enjoying particular popularity. His plays soon obtained a secure place in the Theater an der Wien and on the other suburban stages. Small wonder then that Schubert, for his first attempts at opera (*Der Spiegelritter*, D. 11 (1811) and *Des Teufels Lustschloss*, D. 84), turned to texts by Kotzebue.

After Schikaneder left the Theater an der Wien, opera continued to be the mainstay there, but the new managers did not possess Schikaneder's touch. As box office receipts dwindled, new works were added in hope that variety would stimulate attendance, but the result was a severe financial crisis. A "steering committee," the *Gesellschaft der Kavaliere,* which also managed the National Theaters, was called in but was unable to set matters right. A short-lived turn for the better occurred when, in 1813, Count Palffy took over the direction of the Theater an der Wien. Not a theatrical manager, he literally managed to gamble away his own fortune within a few years. While the National Theaters and the Theater an der Wien shared a common management, many singers were able to make the move to the Kärntnertor Theater. This had forced Palffy to revise the repertory. Up to then opera had been the favored genre: Gluck, Isouard, Gyrowetz, Paër, d'Alayrac, Grétry, Salieri, Cherubini and Boieldieu were regularly performed, along with works by Ignaz Seyfried, the resident composer at the Theater an der Wien. Palffy now had to give preference to the *Singspiel,* a genre to which Seyfried also contributed heavily. Palffy, well aware of the public's fondness for spectacle, presented other kinds of entertainment, soon finding that ballet and pantomime brought excellent box office receipts. Among his innovations were children's ballets in which he invested huge sums and which were enthusiastically received. *Das Waldmädchen* by Horschelt with music by Wranitzky ran for 54 performances, for example. But there were those who contended that the ballets endangered children's morals. At the secret request of the government a police investigation was launched in 1818 to determine whether "it was true that several children, due to overexertion, had contracted and died from lung disease; furthermore, whether a deterioration of morals had been observed among young persons appearing in these ballets."[2] Though the investigation found neither complaint supportable, children's ballets were nevertheless forbidden by imperial decree—a decision which created sensational headlines in the newspapers of the day. But because an important source of income had dried up, Palffy was forced to come up with a sensation of his own: in 1819 he organized a lottery, no doubt a unique event in the annals of Viennese theatrical history, in which, with official approval, the theater was offered as the prize. His plan caused much excitement and immediately became the subject for parodies given in the other suburban theaters: *Die Ausspielung des Theaters* in the Leopoldstadt and *Die letzte Ziehung des Theaters* in the Josefstadt theater.

But no box office successes could equal the success of the lottery itself:

> People fought over the lottery tickets on sale at the Hönikstein Bank in the Kärntnerstrasse. Women who told fortunes from cards did a tremendous business; countless people wanted to know whether it was in the cards that they would win the theater or some other prize. . . . People went without food in order to save enough money for a ticket, every harper from Thury's [part of a suburb, today in the ninth district—tr.], every lantern lighter from the Mehlgrube, every street sweeper already saw himself as Count Palffy's successor. . . . The drawings turned into a kind of public holiday, and the final drawing brought pandemonium. Both the heat and the crowds were unbearable. One waited in vain all morning for the drawing of the first prize. At last the number was announced. The lucky winner turned out to be a wealthy wine merchant from Tyrnau with the "unusual" name of Mayer. He elected to refuse the theater, opting instead for the alternative cash prize of 300,000 Gulden, paid out in shiny 20-Gulden gold pieces.[3]

By this device Palffy had not only become the talk of the town but also did handsomely financially. But the eventual collapse, the result of his continued reckless spending, was inevitable. In December 1826 the theater was sold at public auction.

A decided decline in the quality of presentations had become noticeable years before. Musical comedies and farces (Possen) rather than *Singspiele* dominated the repertory. Hack writers of the day, uninhibited by so much as a nod to literary standards, churned out work after work. They flooded the market, especially the smaller houses, and even saw their hack plays performed at the Theater an der Wien. Among these busy scribblers were Adolf Bäuerle, Carl Meisl, Joseph Alois Gleich and Ignaz Castelli; the occasional music was cranked out by composers of the ilk of Franz Volkert, Vincenz and Ferdinand Tuczek, Franz Roser, Franz Gläser, and finally Joseph

Drechsler and Wenzel Müller, typically on a few days' notice. The popular demand for these musical farces, pantomimes, melodramas and magic plays was insatiable. Many were short-lived, but all offered opportunities to display the theater's sensational technical equipment.

The inexperienced young Schubert marched unwittingly into this mire of third-rate offerings in the hope of establishing himself as an operatic composer. His *Zauberharfe,* (The Magic Harp) D. 644, was conceived in the fashion of the time; the pretentious staging was seen as more important than the music. Under these circumstances one could hardly expect him to succeed as a creditable composer. The work, as required, contains scene after scene of pure melodrama. In general the music is so closely tied to the conventions of the time that it was bound to be short-lived.

The same must be said of *Rosamunde, Fürstin von Zypern,* D. 797, composed to a mediocre libretto by Wilhelmine von Chézy. The piece was called "A Great Romantic Spectacle with Choruses and Dances." The billing alone indicates that music was of distinctly secondary importance. Moreover, the composer was given little time to write it. Schubert, it appears, was expected to share the approach of the authors of comedies and their musical collaborators: music written for stage works demanded no intellectual effort but rather was pure hack work. The management was unprepared to offer the time needed for a well-developed opera project, nor were they interested in such substantial works.

After the several financial crises which had rocked the Theater, long-range planning was impossible. They needed works that would satisfy then and there—in short, they needed "hits."

A composer who could be counted on to supply sure-fire hits was Giacomo Rossini who had first come to the attention of the Viennese in 1816 when *Tancredi* premiered at the National Theater. Palffy quickly decided to give it in his theater. Since his "privilege" extended only to German-language works, it was performed in German in 1817.

Rossini remained the great attraction of the Theater an der Wien through 1821. *Elisabetta, regina d'Inghilterra, Otello, La gazza ladra, Armida, L'Italiana in Algeri, Edoardo e Cristina, Il barbiere di Siviglia, La Cenerentola* and *Mose* were in the repertory, in German, generally before the original versions were presented at the National Theater. These operas were responsible for igniting the "Rossini mania" which, in 1822, developed into veritable hysteria at the National Theater. At first, however, Palffy had stolen the show from the court theater. It is therefore likely that Schubert, of whose attendance and general knowledge of the repertory we know nothing, received his first sense of Rossini's music at the Theater an der Wien. He could not altogether avoid Rossini's influence, though he basically had a negative attitude toward this Italian manner with its constant search for striking effects. Schubert's operatic attempt *Adrast*, D. 137, written late in 1819 or early in 1820,[4] shows elements of Rossini's manner in the passage work and the fairly obvious melodies. To be sure, the thematic treatment is different from Rossini's[5] whose music tends to grow from small groups of motives. But the stereotyped melody patterns found, for instance, in Croesus' area (see illustration on page 68) represent a manner atypical of Schubert and suggest Italian models. One might theorize that Schubert, realizing that he was under the spell of the "Italian craze" then so rampant in Vienna, decided to abandon this operatic project. At least this is one possible reason. Earlier, in 1817, he had written two overtures "In the Italian Style," D. 590 and 591: were they intended as proof, serious or tongue-in-cheek, that he was at home in this idiom? Be this as it may: in the face of Rossini's successes which extended to all segments of musical society, Schubert had to give up. He was not the only composer whose operatic endeavors were frustrated by the rule of the Italians. The success of Weber's *Freischütz* at the Theater an der Wien in 1822 gave those patriotic souls, tiring of the Rossini craze, hope for a break-through of German Romantic opera. This hope was further nourished by the success of Weber's *Preciosa* at the Theater an der Wien in the summer of 1823. But disappointment followed only a few months later with the fiasco of *Euryanthe* at the National Theater. Even Schubert commented on it negatively.[6]

After 1823 neither Rossini nor Weber were played at the Theater an der Wien. The audiences were again satisfied with light, insipid fare—comedies with music by Roser, Philip Jakob Riotte, and occasionally Conradin Kreutzer and Wenzel Müller as well. Plans were made in 1824 once more to invite a contribution from Schubert. He was to set a libretto entitled *Der kurze Mantel,* written by the prolific, patriotic writer, Johann Gabriel Seidl. Schubert was later to describe him as lacking any poetic talent.[7] Most likely it was the poor quality of the text that dissuaded him, rather than the thought of being performed in a theater that was going downhill. In his place Riotte, Joseph v. Blumenthal and Seyfried together supplied music for Seidl's libretto. They were rewarded by ten performances at the Theater an der Wien.

Schubert had no direct connections to the other suburban theaters. In October 1826 he attended a performance of *Aline* by Bäuerle and Wenzel Müller at the Leopoldstadt Theater, which he had most likely visited before.[8] It had the reputation of being the most important, German-language, popular theater in Vienna. Its repertory satisfied not only modest local expectations with light

Franz Schubert. Original drawing by Moritz v. Schwind

Page from the autograph score of Schubert's unfinished opera *Adrast*: Aria of Krösus

Illustration from title page of a collection of dance music published by Sauer &
Leidesdorf, Vienna. Caricature of Schubert (standing)

69

wird

Leopold Jansa,

Mitglied der k. k. Hofkapelle,

Sonntag den 22. April 1827, um die Mittagsstunde,

i m

Saale der n. ö. Herren Landstände,

e i n

Concert

zu geben, die Ehre haben.

Vorkommende Stücke:

1. Ouverture aus Egmont von Ludwig van Beethoven.

2. Adagio und Rondo für zwey Violinen concertant, componirt vom Concertgeber; vorgetragen von Ebendemselben, und Herrn Feigerl.

3. Norman's Gesang von Walter Scott, in Musik gesetzt von Herrn Fr. Schubert, vorgetragen von einem ausgezeichneten Sänger, begleitet auf dem Pianoforte vom Compositeur selbst.

4. Trio aus E-dur von Hummel, der Fortepianopart vorgetragen von Herrn Carl M. von Bocklet.

5. Deklamation von Dem. Müller, k. k. Hofschauspielerinn.

6. Neue Variationen, komponirt und vorgetragen vom Concertgeber.

Aus besonderer Gefälligkeit für den Concertgeber haben Dem. Müller, und die oben benannten Herren Künstler ihre Parten, so wie Herr Franz, Mitglied der k. k. Hofkapelle, die Leitung des Orchesters bereitwillig übernommen.

Eintrittskarten zu drey Gulden W. W. sind in den Kunst- und Musikalienhandlungen der Herren Haslinger, und Pennauer am Graben, so wie am Tage der Aufführung an der Cassa zu haben.

Der Anfang ist um halb ein Uhr.

Concert program: second performance of *Norman's Gesang,* D.846 in a concert given by the violinist Leopold Jansa. The "ausgezeichnete Sänger" (distinguished singer) was Ludwig Tietze.

opera, musical comedy and farce, but included the more substantial *Singspiel* as well. The quality of performance was not always of the best, but a greater variety was offered than could be found in any comparable theaters. Before 1812 the management had occasionally looked to foreign models and arranged Grétry, Méhul and D'Alayrac for the requirements of the popular theater; after that date almost without exception domestic works were given. The resident conductor/composer was Wenzel Müller who had joined the company in 1786, coming from Brünn. Ferdinand Kauer was the second-in-command; his *Donauweibchen* had achieved lasting popularity. According to contemporary reports Schubert thought highly of Müller whose large oeuvre was devoted exclusively to the stage. He dominated the musical scene at the Leopoldstadt Theater for decades. Singspiele (*Neusonntagskind*), comic operas (*Der Fiaker als Marquis*), magic operas (*Aline*) flowed from his pen, along with music for fairy tales (*Die Teufelsmühle am Wienerberg*) and parodies of works that had achieved the status of classics (*Die neue Alzeste; Die travestierte Zauberflöte*). Many of these pieces were kept in the permanent repertory. His position of leadership was uncontested until about 1825 when Joseph Drechsler became a serious rival.

Few other outstanding composers were associated with the Leopoldstadt Theater during Schubert's lifetime. A group of versatile musicians was always available, ready to supply pleasant music on demand and on short notice, an arrangement similar to that under which the poets Bäuerle, Gleich and Meisl worked for the same theater. Ignaz Schuster, Tuczek, Volkert, Roser and Jakob Haibel did this kind of work for some 20 years. They were joined around 1820 by Franz Gläser. It stands to reason that working steadily under such conditions made it difficult to avoid falling into uninspired routine. It was a stroke of luck that Ferdinand Raimund became a member of the company in 1817 and that two years later Drechsler achieved a spectacular success with his magic play *Der Berggeist,* his first work for the Leopoldstadt Theater.

Raimund had gained his stage experience at the Josefstadt Theater. As an actor (he also was a fine musician) he played the lead parts in the routine plays of Meisl and Bäuerle. Finally no longer able to stomach this "garbage" and "hack work:"[9] he in 1823 began writing himself. He turned to Wenzel Müller for music for his *Barometermacher auf der Zauberinsel* while Drechsler was asked to compose *Der Diamant des Geisterkö*nigs and *Das Mädchen aus der Feenwelt.*

In Raimund's works we notice a turn away from the usual farces in favor of magic and fairy plays. He also excelled in spectacular costume and makeup changes. *Das Mädchen aus der Feenwelt* became his most popular play; for some years it was claimed that Schubert had collaborated on the music. Certainly Schubert showed an interest in the genre and quite possibly saw this successful piece. But to this day no proof has been found of any collaboration with Drechsler. The mere resemblance of Wurzel's aria to Schubert's *Trauerwalzer,* D. 365/2, is insufficient evidence.

Unfortunately, hypotheses and untruths have always been part of the Schubert literature—untruths that tend to go back to various statements from Schubert's circle of friends. Josef Hüttenbrenner, for instance, was a self-proclaimed authority in these matters; he claimed that in 1822 the director of the recently built Josefstadt Theater had promised him to perform Schubert's youth opera, *Des Teufels Lustschloss,* D. 84. Now Vienna could point with pride to the fact that this theater had been inaugurated with Beethoven's overture *Die Weihe des Hauses,* specially composed for the occasion—but there is no indication whatever that Schubert had any ties to the theater.[10] Quite possibly he attended some performances there, even before it was rebuilt, but the repertory did not differ substantially from what one could see and hear at the other suburban theaters. The many farces, parodies, quodlibets, burlesques and *Ritterspiele,* along with popular plays by Kotzebue and, later, ballets, left little room for opera or *Singspiel.* The Josefstadt Theater attracted attention when a new Grillparzer work was given its first performance— *Die Ahnfrau* in May 1817 or *Sappho* in June 1826—but these were rare, special events. An arrangement made with the Kärntnertor Theater (1825/26) to provide guest engagements for Josefstadt artists heightened the prestige and inspired the management to reintroduce a few operas, at least for a short time. Rossini's *Barber of Seville* and *La Gazza Ladra* were given, as was Weber's *Der Freischütz*—but the undertaking ended there.

Franz Gläser, the resident Kapellmeister at the Josefstadt Theater, was a composer of many farces, *Zauberspiele,* and pantomimes. His attitude toward opera was strange, to put it mildly. The first performance of Weber's *Oberon* (March 1827) demonstrated his lack of musical judgement. He gave the title role to the comedian Wenzel Scholz, which caused much unintended laughter. He also "arranged" the opera for this stage by obtaining a vocal score and giving free rein to his blue pencil. Nor did he hesitate to add to Weber's music. He rewrote the text in *Knittelvers* (doggerel) the predictable result of which was general and critical consternation. Everyone was indignant, and this *Oberon,* announced as "Weber's masterpiece," was quickly removed from the repertory.[11]

For a young composer, still unsure about his dramatic music objectives, the state of the suburban theaters was far from promising. Schubert tended toward the *Singspiel,* as exemplified by his *Fernando,* D. 220, *Die Freunde von Salamanka,* D. 326, *Der vierjährige Posten,* D. 190

and others. He seems to have been discouraged from pursuing this course farther due to the run-of-the-mill output expected by the managers. If he tried to supply what was currently in favor, as in the case of his *Zauberharfe,* D. 644, he fared no better than the others who wrote for immediate consumption: the works soon went out of fashion, and after a few performances disappeared forever.

Schubert really wished to write grand opera and particularly German Romantic opera. But those in authority showed little interest or understanding.

The evolution of the Kärntnertor Theater also presented obstacles to the realization of Schubert's operatic intentions. While still at the *Konvikt* he was able to listen not only to performances of works by Gluck (*Armida, Alceste*), Grétry, Méhul, Cherubini, Paër, Spontini, and Mozart (*La clemenza di Tito, The Magic Flute*) but also *Singspiele* (by Gyrowetz, Isouard, Boieldieu) and operettas by Ignaz Mosel. However, following the separation of the Kärntnertor Theater and Burgtheater in 1810 significant changes in repertory occurred in both. The former house presented only operas and ballets but at a price to the music-loving public, as "only German works, being the true national entertainment" for which "the lowest possible admission prices"[12] were required, were presented. Quickly the theater announced ballets and divertissements, indicating that the management was prepared to cater to the public's desire for lighter entertainment. This was welcome fare for the Congress of Vienna participants: amusements of all kinds were in demand. Similar entertainments were also supplied by the National Theater with works labelled "Pantomimisches Ballet," "Anakreontisches Ballet," "Ländliches [rustic] Ballet," or just "Divertissement." The Congress even seemed to shape the 1815 season; only rarely did one of the theaters bill grand operas by Catel, Méhul and Isouard, and no effort was made to cultivate German opera.

In 1816, Anton Cera, "Director and Manager of the Italian Opera Company," scheduled several Italian operas. Encouraged by his success he expanded the offerings yearly so that by late in 1821 only Italian operas were presented. Before this change Schubert was, thanks to the help of the singer Johann Michael Vogl, given the opportunity to try his hand at an opera on the stage of the National Theater. His one-acter *Die Zwillingsbrüder*, D. 647, which he himself labelled *Posse*, would have been more appropriate for one of the suburban theaters than for the National Theater. Schubert purportedly drafted the work as early as January 1819, on commission, but had not carried it further. He would have been better off not offering the score to the court theater. By then he already had written several Singspiele and drafted a three-act opera, *Die Bürgschaft*, D. 435. Its ludicrous text, by an unknown author, based on the same subject as Schiller's poem, should have been thoroughly revised. To judge by the quality of the existing portions of the score one regrets that it was not finished. It is possible that *Adrast*, D. 137, rather than the *Zwillingsbrüder*, had been intended for the Kärntnertor Theater, but that Schubert, for reasons indicated above, changed his mind.[13] At any rate, an unusually long time elapsed between the commission, if indeed there was an official commission, and performance, which suggests several possible explanations. Perhaps Schubert procrastinated but eventually was pushed by his friends, especially by Vogl who had a double role in *Zwillingsbrüder* and who would have welcomed a good role just before leaving the National Theater. We learn from the diaries of Josef Karl Rosenbaum that Schubert's friends genuinely promoted the work, but that Schubert chose not to attend the opening.[14]

Late in 1821 Domenico Barbaja, the impresario with a dubious reputation acquired in Milan and Naples, took over the Kärntnertor Theater. The following spring he launched a highly successful series of Rossini operas. *Donna del Lago, La Cenerentola, Zelmira, Il Corradino,* and *Elisabetta* were all given in quick succession. As the crowning glory Barbaja brought Rossini to Vienna, for a *stagione* in April, 1822.

The main requirement for a "good" opera was that it must be "pleasant." Such standards made it clear that German opera did not have a chance. Still, Barbaja was sufficiently clever to make a conciliatory gesture in the direction of German opera. Weber's *Freischütz* had been extremely well received in Vienna in 1821. Barbaja therefore commissioned Weber to write another opera, *Euryanthe,* which had its first performance in October 1823. It was an artistic failure, a disappointment for both the composer and the National Theater. Following this Barbaja operated with greater caution, which worked to Schubert's disadvantage. According to an unconfirmed story Barbaja, through Joseph Kupelwieser, the then secretary of the Kärntnertor Theater, commissioned Schubert to write an opera. Kupelwieser was an aspiring writer himself. If indeed he was the go-between he saw to it that the libretto would be his. It is true that from spring to fall 1823 Schubert worked on the three-act opera *Fierabras,* D. 796, its text based on an old French tale. The manuscript copy of Kupelwieser's libretto[15] and the *Wiener Allgemeine Theaterzeitung* indicate that a performance at the Kärntnertor Theater had been planned.[16] On November 29, 1823 it was announced that 'Fierobras [sic] will be postponed for the time being." This postponement may have been related to the failure of *Euryanthe* four weeks earlier. Writing to Leopold Kupelwieser, brother of the "poet," Schubert mentioned that the libretto had been declared "unacceptable."[17] To his friend Schober he hinted at other reasons for the rejection: Kupelwieser's departure from the Kärntnertor Theater and disagreements between Barbaja and Palffy who had given Barbaja the concession for the Theater an der Wien as well. He wrote to Schober:

> Things are going badly with my two operas [the other being *Alfonso und Estrella*]. Kupelwieser suddenly left the theater; Weber's *Euryanthe* did not turn out well and was poorly received—rightly so, I think. These circumstances, and a falling out between Barbaja and Palffy, cause me to give up hope for my opera. Actually it is just as well, since performances are so poor these days.[18]

From the last remark one gains the impression that Schubert had followed developments at the Kärntnertor closely and that he had attended some performances. Though his criticism was primarily directed at the performances it may also have applied to the poor quality of the repertory. Save for Rossini, and Mozart's *La clemenza di Tito* and *Figaro,* the 1823 season offered gems such as: *Der junge Onkel,* an operetta by Schoberlechner; *Paul und Rosette,* a rustic ballet by Corally; *Die Rose,* also a rustic ballet by a composer named Henry who also contributed an anacreontic ballet *Paris;* the romantic fairy ballet *Ismaans Grab;* and the heroic ballet *Die Amazonen.* One might also have seen performances of *Das Ständchen,* a Singspiel by Gyrowetz; *Cordelia,* a "lyric-tragic opera" by Kreutzer; the melodrama *Abufa* by Carafa; a pastoral play with music by Weigl *Nachtigall und Rabe;* etc.

Such programming was hardly worthy of a national theater, even during this period. Schubert may indeed have been offended by having been turned down in favor of such offerings, despite his efforts to put himself into Barbaja's good graces. At the very time Schubert submitted his *Fierabras* to the Kärntnertor management Barbaja was celebrating his own name day for which a suitable serenade, *Nachtmusik auf der Bastei,* was performed to honor the occasion. Schubert contributed a vocal quartet, *Die Nachtigall,* D. 724, which "pleased the most."[19] But even this show of good will on Schubert's part did not change Barbaja's negative decision. There was no hope for Schubert as long as Barbaja was in charge.

Following Barbaja's resignation the theater was closed for a short period after which, in late April 1826, Ignaz Mosel was appointed director. He had the reputation of being an advocate of German opera. But not everyone approved of the expected change in repertory. Karl Freiherr von Schönstein was a Schubert acquaintance and a gifted singer, completely devoted to Italian opera until he discovered the beauty of Schubert's *Lieder.* At the time the two of them returned to Vienna from Zselitz he made known his unhappiness with the anticipated change at the Kärntnertor Theater. He made no bones about the kind of theater he preferred:

> I had hardly arrived in Vienna when I heard the news, unfortunately true, that Barbaja's lease was to end on December 1. There may be singers whose contracts extend beyond this—but since Barbaja's lease will expire and since the theater will be completely closed down there is no hope that we might have Italian opera this winter. One might put up with the lack of German opera—it would have been hard to take after the Italian ones—but no more ballets (which means that my dear Rosier is lost to me forever): that really hurts.[20]

During Mosel's directorship of both court theaters (a purely nominal appointment) Schubert supposedly applied for the position of Vice Court Kapellmeister at the Kärntnertor Theater. One can add this legend to the many other "historical facts" that were bandied about by Beethoven's biographer Anton Schindler.[21] The appointment was surely discussed in the Schubert circle; perhaps friends even urged Schubert to apply—but it is inconceivable that, having no theatrical experience whatever, he should have been interested in such a position. What is more, he must have known the kind of repertory he, as second Kapellmeister, would have been expected to rehearse. From the summer of 1826 to the spring of 1827 the National Theater brought in French vaudevilles by Scribe, Delavigne, Désaugiers, Mélesville and others. Subsequently German opera (Spohr) and *Singspiel* were gradually returned to the repertory, after which the first great successes of Donizetti and Bellini were staged.

Nothing in Schubert's relation to the National Theater changed during Mosel's tenure. He continued to be ignored as a dramatic composer. Still, the gradual ebbing of Rossini's popularity probably encouraged him to tackle another stage work. With the librettist Eduard Bauernfeld a subject was chosen, but *Der Graf von Gleichen*, D. 918, was no literary masterpiece—small wonder, in view of Bauernfeld's inferior models. Since the subject involved bigamy there were other troubles: the libretto was not approved by the government censors. Schubert, still fascinated by the subject, decided to compose the opera anyway, hoping that influential friends would straighten out the problem.

This opera, of which we know less than of Schubert's other stage works (it remained a fragment), does indeed hold a special place. It exists in the form of a piano sketch, lacking the overture and the last two numbers which remained unwritten.[22] Among the known Schubert manuscripts piano sketches are rare; most of the extant documents stem from his last years. He seems to have chosen such a format when he was experimenting—when working in a genre in which he did not feel secure. Certainly this is conjecture; it might be refuted if we had more manuscripts that show how Schubert worked with sketches. In the symphonic field he admittedly was "feeling his way;" he proceeded likewise, though unfortunately with less success, in opera. *Der Graf von Gleichen* occupied him more intensively than any of his earlier stage works. We can believe Bauernfeld's statement that it absorbed Schubert until his death—that is to say, more than a year, and that his manner of sketching was unusual. It seems that he carried sketches with him at all times, or at least for a long period of time, as though he wanted to use every available moment to work on it. The manuscript consists of several sections, written on sheets of varying sizes, which also suggests that he did not work on it continuously.

The manuscript of this opera convincingly disproves the all too familiar cliché that Schubert had only to sit down, pen in hand, to produce instantly page after page of finished music.

Der Graf von Gleichen is eloquent proof of Schubert's intention to come to terms with grand Romantic opera. Regrettably he left but a sketch, though it is a product of his mature years. In it he demonstrated a fine sense for ensemble writing. He also stressed dramatically effective solo singing over more lyrical, Lied-like elements.

Schubert and Dance Music

The early 19th century saw many changes in society, including changes in social life. In Vienna these changes were especially evident in the world of public dances; their great number and popularity were an expression of *joie de vivre* in spite of the depressing political climate of the time. Traditionally the Viennese preferred "baroque" life styles, greatly enjoying all that was exaggerated and sensational. It therefore comes as no surprise that in spite of their distinct social positions the nobility and commoners shared the pleasures of the multitude of entertainments that were available. Foreigners often criticized or made fun of this Viennese passion for enjoying life to the fullest.

The lavishly appointed Apollo Ballrooms opened their doors in 1808 and provided just the right setting for the 19th-century explosion in public dancing. Johann Friedrich Reichardt visiting the city in 1809 was amazed by these doings; he could not comprehend that even the Napoleonic threat failed to put a damper on all this:

> This huge, splendid, extremely luxurious entertainment center was conceived and built by someone who was not Viennese. It is located far from the center of town, in a suburb with unpaved streets, so that during the winter months it is accessible by carriage only. There is no place like it in all of Europe. The cost of admission is twice the amount that had been customary for such entertainments; the facilities for wining and dining are

elegant . . . In spite of the prices the Apollo Ballrooms are very popular. There have been evenings when 7–8000 people filled the place to capacity. Only about a tenth of those belong to the upper class. One can see entire families from the lower middle class, landowners and tenant farmers from the surrounding countryside, with their families. Even servants from city and country join the crowds that fill the many halls and smaller rooms which are splendidly decorated and illuminated, ringing with the sound of music.[1]

Even members of Europe's ruling houses who attended the Congress of Vienna knew how to appreciate what was offered; they seemed to consider it not beneath their dignity to rub elbows with the common crowd. Count de la Garde, an alert observer, did not fail to report that "crowned heads" pursued their pleasures with members of the lower classes:

While the countryside was covered with snow, inside the establishment a spring-like atmosphere prevailed with warmth and scented air. On entering we were impressed by the size of the crowd . . . I must admit that at the official entertainments of the Congress one did not meet such a festive crowd, coming from all walks of life. . . . A memorable spectacle; a little world of its own. Since they could attend incognito, members of royalty much preferred these informal entertainments to the court balls with their elaborate ceremonial.[2]

The number and variety of opportunities to dance in Vienna were indeed impressive. Anyone able to pay the price of admission was free to attend the public balls, the *Redouten.* Then there were dancing parties given by members of society, open by invitation only. The dancing parties in private homes often also involved games and costumes. Masked balls were permitted only if the masks and costumes met approved standards of "decency." Public masquerades, so popular elsewhere, were officially discouraged out of fear that masked processions and parades might get out of hand,[3] which explains why a tradition of masked balls never developed in Vienna.

82

The number of establishments offering such entertainments steadily increased in the early 19th century, partly because establishments permitted to serve alcoholic beverages were also permitted to offer dance music about this time. By 1820 things had gotten to the point where the police decided some control was necessary.

> There now are so many taverns employing dance musicians, especially in the suburbs, that it no longer seems advisable to tie permits for dancing to the issuance of a beverage license. Because this was done in the past, dancing establishments have mushroomed, and with them all kinds of disorderly conduct and other excesses, all to the detriment of nocturnal peace and quiet.[4]

I have mentioned the elegant Redoutensaal and the elaborate "Pleasure Establishment," the Apollosaal on the Schottenfeld which burned down in 1815 but was rebuilt. In addition there were the *Sperlsäle* in the Leopoldstadt and several inns: *Zum Mondenschein* near the Karlskirche; *Zu den zwey Täuberln,* and *Zum Schwarzen Bock* on the Wieden, where Josef Lanner held forth. The *Mondschein* or *Langaus Ballroom* was located next to the house where Schubert and his friend Moritz v. Schwind lived in 1825.[5] This hall became famous about 1800 when "Langaus dancers" congregated there. The "Langaus" was a particular form of the waltz: one couple gyrated around the room's periphery,[6] continually increasing the speed of their mad whirl. These "excesses" were soon forbidden by the police, after contemporary critics pointed to the gravity of the situation:

> Ten to eleven thousand deaths occur annually in Vienna. The cause of death for about one-fourth of these is consumption which can be brought on by immoderate waltzing.[7]

But the Viennese craze for the waltz was not to be ended by police edicts. This "new-fangled" dance was at first greeted with some reserve and in aristocratic circles largely ignored. It was forbidden at the German courts for some years while in France the devotees of the waltz were threatened with the refusal of absolution. But in Vienna the initial reserve soon vanished. The festivities of the Congress of Vienna would have been unthinkable without it. By that time it was danced as we do today. No one seemed able to escape its fascination, and once more Count de la Garde, chronicler of the Congress, was the attentive observer:

> After Their Majesties had left, the orchestra began playing waltzes. The crowd at once seemed electrified. . . . It is difficult to understand the powerful effect of the waltz. As soon as the first notes are heard everyone's eyes light up: a feeling of delight overcomes one and all. The couples start gyrating like tops, moving forward, crossing in front of and passing each other. . . . Only with the end of night does the frenzy end; only the first rays of the sun cause the lively party to break up.[8]

Scholars remain uncertain about the origin of the term "Viennese waltz," and recent studies have paid more attention to the etymology than to the musical characteristics.[9] At any rate, composers of the time and their publishers used the term routinely on the title pages of their dances.

Mozart, Haydn and Beethoven wrote dance music, usually on commission, for use at the Redouten balls. Their contributions, consisting mostly of minuets and *Deutsche,* conformed to courtly requirements. Such conservative compositions offered no likelihood of offending the conventions of society; no aristocratic guest could be offended by excesses. But Vienna also attracted countless composers from the far corners of the empire (among them Stanislaus d'Ossowsky, a Polish composer extremely successful in Vienna) who were unconcerned about court etiquette and so quite willing to write dance music for the people. We can trace a popular dance form from the *Deutsche* (chiefly from Bavaria) by way of the Ländler to the waltz. As in other times and with other interests, Vienna had proved to be the place where ideas and practices arising elsewhere were assimilated. Quite likely the waltz, in a still primitive and vulgar form, was a part of the repertory of the so-called "Linz fiddlers." Such groups played Ländler (usually for two violins and bass) in Upper Austria, late in the 18th century, and during the next decades brought them to Vienna where they could be heard in the inns along the Danube and in suburban taverns. In just such a setting they were played by the "band" of Michael Pamer in which Josef Lanner "grew up."

Schubert began writing Ländler early in 1816. The instrumentation he chose points to these suburban models. Ländler D. 354, 355, 370 and 374 are scored for one or two violins. It is possible that the Ländler calling for only one violin simply reflect the loss of the second violin part. The same is true of the bass part which tended to be so standardized that it was hardly necessary to write it down. This uncertainty is a general problem in dance research: improvisation has always been important in playing dance music, so the exact line of descent, from the *Deutsche* to the waltz, is only partially traceable.

Neither *Deutsche* nor waltz figure prominently among the works of composers of "serious" music, as is true of Schubert whose contributions to either are very limited. At his time the waltz simply was not yet considered "fit for society," and even at the "Schubertiads" dancing the conventional *Deutsche* was preferred. There is no indication that waltzes figured importantly at their gatherings. After Schubert's early attempt in 1816, his subsequent Ländler, when he indeed used that name, are piano compositions, two-hand or four-hand, and are rather stylized.

Beginning in 1811, when only in his early teens, Schubert's dance music was largely confined to minuets, but late in 1813 the term minuet gradually disappears from the titles he placed on his compositions. Now the *Deutsche* takes precedence, and after 1815 another dance form which gained popularity: the Ecossaise. It is an old Scottish dance which Beethoven still wrote in triple time while Schubert's are in lively duple time. Ecossaises must have been a great favorite in Schubert's circle, judging by its prominence at the "Schubertiads" and in the catalogue of Schubert's works. Undoubtedly he improvised others, in keeping with common practice at the time, but never committed them to paper.

Great importance has been attached to Schubert's dance music, some scholars attributing to him a crucial role in the evolution of the waltz.[10] True, he left us a large number of charming dances, but he seemed to view them as purely utilitarian music. He paid very little attention to their publication. The music publishers printed them, in collections which bore no relation to their time of composition and their quality. These collections were published with fanciful titles that were likely not supplied by the composer. Schubert also contributed to collections of dances intended for the carnival season, among them *Neue Krähwinkler Tänze, Halt's enk z'sam,* and *Moderne Liebes-Walzer.* In these he joined company of such composers as Pensel, Czapek, Lanz, Fischhof, Sowinsky and others whose talents were limited to the requirements of trivial entertainment music.

The development of the waltz, especially that still called the Viennese waltz, did not involve Schubert. As noted earlier, Josef Lanner (born in Vienna in 1801) and his mentor Michael Pamer deserve credit for that development. Lanner modestly pointed to Carl Maria von Weber as the composer responsible for fashioning this typically Viennese dance. Weber's *Aufforderung zum Tanz* (Invitation to the Dance), written in 1819 and reprinted by

Diabelli in 1824, established the form which later came to characterize the concert waltz: an introduction with motivic material anticipating the dance itself, and a musically elaborate coda. Lanner used both in his own *Aufforderung zum Tanz*, named after Weber's, and in which the construction of the coda is of particular interest. Lanner did not hesitate in adding his own Ländler to Weber's principal melodies. Lanner's *Aufforderung* was published as Op. 7, and followed by his *Mitternachts-Walzer* (Midnight-Waltz), his first work to be entitled "waltz." In it the "chain of waltzes" was reduced from 12 to 5. Such formal tightening indicates that greater emphasis was now put on the waltz as art music; before this composers, such as Hummel, had written what seemed to be endless chains of waltzes.[11]

Lanner's star was rising: he enlarged his ensemble and moved to a location in the center of Vienna, the inn *Zum Rebhuhn*, where Schubert is reported to have heard him. Our information about contacts between Schubert and Lanner is hearsay; Lanner may have attended one of the performances of Schubert's *Zauberharfe* and praised its overture. Though it cannot be proved, Schubert probably heard of the disagreements between Lanner and Johann Strauss, Sr. which led to their parting of the ways. After all, this episode was the talk of the town; why should it not have reached Schubert?

In May 1827 the proprietor of the inn *Zu den zwey Täuberln* announced that "a full orchestra composed of 12 string and wind players and directed by Herr Johann Strauss" would play in his establishment. Possibly Schubert was among the patrons. His only proven connection with Strauss and Lanner is contained in an advertisement in Diabelli's collection of "Favorite Viennese Dances," published as *Der musikalische Gesellschafter in einsamen Stunden, für eine Flöte eingerichtet* (The Music

Companion for Lonely Hours, Arranged for Flute). The three composers also appear in Haslinger's *Neue Faschingsspenden* (New Carnival Gifts) where Schubert is included as a composer of dances.

From all this it should be evident that the waltz, its origin and early stages, had little to do with the musical life of the upper middle class. Nor can we imagine such dance music to have developed out of music-making in the home, or from *Biedermeier* entertainments involving music. Dance music relies too much on popular appeal; it is intended to captivate also those who have no other musical interests or understanding. Lanner, and especially the ambitious Johann Strauss, Sr., soon realized the nature of their public and wrote dances which in their topical allusions went far beyond anything that had been done before. Their concern with what was then in vogue is reflected not only in topical subject matter, documented by titles from the 1820s such as *Vermählungswalzer* (Wedding Waltz, Lanner) and *Kettenbrückenwalzer* (Strauss' first great success, written for the opening of Vienna's second chain bridge) but also by the simple musical style employed. Thus popular elements from Italian and French opera as well as tunes from German *Singspiele* were depended upon to introduce new melodic and formal aspects into dance music. Strauss and Lanner were experts at this; they well knew what would succeed with the public. They did not ignore "folk" and popular music, but they also borrowed from "art" music. That their artistic aims were high is also shown by their evolving manner of orchestration which became increasingly "classical," i.e., symphonic. In this way the waltz gained admission to the aristocratic world. Recognition was not long in coming: only a year after Schubert's death Lanner was appointed Music Director of the Imperial and Royal Redoutensäle.

The Literary Scene

The amount of scholarly writing about the "Pre-March" period in Vienna [the period before the revolution in March 1848—tr.] is growing steadily. It was a period, the beginning and end of which, like Romanticism are variously defined. Reviews of the literature of this period unfailingly point to Grillparzer, Raimund and Nestroy as its protagonists. Schubert's lifespan largely coincides with theirs, yet he felt obliged to look elsewhere for literary models or sources—meaning, chiefly, the texts for his songs. Grillparzer's lyric writing did not inspire him; he thought of Raimund chiefly as an actor and viewed Nestroy primarily as a singer, but one whose bass voice was eminently suited for Schubert's vocal quartets. During the years of his first great songs he seems to have had no connection with Grillparzer.

Schubert's interest in literature began at the time when German Romanticism made its appearance in Vienna, an appearance that was watched with apprehension by Austrian officialdom. Emperor Francis I established a system of censorship which revealed not only his limited horizon but his ignorance of cultural matters in particular. These control measures were intended to thwart any revolutionary activities in Austria including those which might affect her intellectual life. Eduard Bauernfeld at a later date rightfully criticized the government for its hostility to education and intellectual growth in its clear intention to isolate Austria from foreign influences.[1] This official suppression of artistic and intellectual activities and values inevitably resulted in Munich and Berlin outclassing Vienna in nurturing and developing a strong literary tradition. Prince Metternich, though commonly said to have had an open mind relative to cultural matters, insisted on absolute control of all media of communication including not only the press, the theater, and publishing in general. In his view literature had at best to mirror his politically reactionary point of view, or at least "defuse" political and social issues. He not only discredited classical literature but also the writings of German idealism. Yet a clever diplomat, he successfully presented himself as the protector and friend of scholarship. As Herbert Seidler, the literary historian, put it: "He kept an eye on the community of recognized scholars. Their access to reading matter was not restricted by censorship since they stood under surveillance anyway."[2] The system of censorship was entirely directed to well-known writers, philosophers, and theologians. The growing ranks of fiction writers were less affected; apparently the censors were too busy to deal with them.

Yet the censors could also be tolerant. Their ranks included educated officials who were not afraid to use their own judgment; they were largely able to distinguish between what was valuable in literature and what was not; that which was harmless and that which was seditious. Though censorship surely imposed restrictions, the daily life of the time was bearable, according to the present-day historian Mikoletzky:

> Things were not all that grim in Austria. No one was forced to leave the country, and censorship usually was involved ex post facto, with conditions stipulated in a typically Austrian, graceful manner. One knew how to make unpleasant things palatable—at the least one knew how to state them in a kind of bureaucratic lan-

90

guage that no one could understand.[3]

Censorship was markedly eased during the French occupation of 1809 resulting in a veritable flood of publications, particularly reprints of the classics. In 1810 Anton Strauss published Goethe's *Collected Writings;* during the same year Anton Doll issued a "Complete Edition" of Schiller's poetry. A particularly significant event helped to stimulate the general interest in literature: a series of public lectures on old and new German literature, given by Friedrich Schlegel in 1812 in the ballroom of the *Römischer Kaiser,* under the protection of the police.[4] Among those attending were a number of the nobility as well as the poets Eichendorff, Matthäus von Collin, and Theodor Körner. These lectures were among the most important literary events of the time. From 1808 to 1829 Schlegel intermittently lived in Vienna, and maintained close contact with Caroline Pichler. The stimulating effect he had on Austrian literature can hardly be exaggerated. Furthermore he had easy access to the imperial court in which he first held the post of court secretary. During the war with France he edited the army newspaper. He then worked for Metternich on matters relating to press policies. This led to the founding of the *Österreichische Beobachter* (The Austrian Observer), the official government journal. Schlegel also used this publication for his own literary purposes, calling attention to Goethe and Schiller, especially to their poetry. Through the *Beobachter* Schlegel greatly influenced the intellectual life of Austria; one is justified in saying that he acquainted Austria with German literature. Literature was the essence of intellectual activity in Schlegel's view.

He was not alone in his efforts to acquaint Vienna's intelligentsia with the literature of the Enlightenment. By moving to the Austrian capital he had set an example followed by other major figures, though for some Vienna was only a way station. Theodor Körner arrived in 1811 and remained until his death. Eichendorff came to study in 1811, while Clemens Brentano resided in the city from 1813 to 1814, with important literary consequences for the city. Brentano's reviews of performances of Schiller's *Kabale und Liebe* and *Die Braut von Messina* appealed to the literary conscience of his contemporaries and led them to come to terms with classic literature.

Metternich and his censors were no doubt suspicious of such eloquent support for the cause of classicism, but after 1809 it did not seem wise to pull up on the reins of censorship: that was to occur after the Congress of Vienna and noticeably following the Karlsbad meetings of 1819. Brentano became the central figure in a literary-religious group that served as a rallying place for young Romantics. They eventually published their views in the journal *Friedensblätter, eine Zeitschrift für Leben, Literatur und Kunst* which existed for only one year. Its contributors included Christian Stolberg, the brother of Count Friedrich Leopold von Stolberg, some of whose texts were composed by Schubert, and Friedrich de la Motte Fouqué, whose novel *Zauberring* of 1813 inspired Schubert to write the three Romanzen *Don Gayseros,* D.93.

Another religiously oriented group gathered around Clemens Maria Hofbauer, a native of Czechoslovakia, which included the preacher Zacharias Werner, highly praised by Friedrich Schlegel. Werner had arrived in Vienna in 1814 soon becoming "fashionable."[5] Hofbauer and his group were intent on "liberating the church from its ties to the spirit of Josephinism."[6] They attracted a large following in Vienna, which was reason enough for Metternich to place them under close surveillance, for Metternich was no friend of the church. The strictly religious orientation of these groups, however, led to only a minimal interest in literary matters. Schubert's loose ties to the Catholic church,[7] resulted in little interest in the religious-spiritual activities of the Hofbauer circle, though he did base some songs on texts by Werner; a good example of Schubert's approach to intellectual matters.

During the first two decades of the 19th century, Viennese intellectual life, insofar as serious literature was concerned, was shaped by German-speaking non-Austrians. Though biographers continue to harp on Schubert's lack of a thorough education, he obviously knew well how to turn this literary efflorescence to his advantage: witness the poems which he set to music. Whether the taste and insight guiding his choice were kindled by his teachers at the *Konvikt* or by his friends is of little importance. The significant factors are the extent to which he made use of contemporary literature and that he felt able to chose freely from a broad spectrum of literary work. Quite understandably he did not restrict himself to "masterworks" but also followed the taste of his time which favored writers such as Kotzebue. This wide-ranging assemblage is clear testimony to his familiarity with the corpus of German literature.

The Viennese publisher Anton Doll began issuing Kotzebue's complete works in 1810, an undertaking finally resulting in 56 volumes in the following 10 years. *Der Spiegelritter,* D.11, and *Des Teufels Lustschloss,* D.84, were published in volumes 3 (1810) and 17 (1811) respectively. (It might be noted that the rate at which this series appeared is an indication of Kotzebue's popularity among the theater-loving Viennese.) Schubert composed these texts soon after their publication. At the age of 14 or 17 he surely was unable to understand Kotzebue's literary intentions. Nor could he understand the sure-fire formula upon which Kotzebue constructed his popular plays and his knightly and middle-class dramas. These plays never failed to impress and attract audiences; many composers tested their musico-dramatic skills with them. "No one knew better how to appeal to the tastes of the common people, how to flatter an audience, how to provide an actor with effective lines."[8]

Schubert's settings of texts by the German poet Friedrich von Matthisson, a disciple of Klopstock and Hölty, were also concessions to popular taste. At about the same time Schubert began to concern himself with Schiller's works, possibly as a result of the esteem in which Schiller held some of Matthisson's writing. Schubert's involvement with the latter lasted from 1812 to 1816 and beyond, but his most intensive preoccupation with Matthisson dates from 1813–1814, a time when his poems had not yet been published in Vienna. Schubert had to fall back on an edition that had appeared in Zürich.

On the other hand, Schubert did have access to the Schiller edition published in Vienna in 1810. Vienna's growing enthusiasm for Schiller extended to the city's principal stage, the Burgtheater, where Schiller's dramas were presented on the recommendation of Josef Schreyvogel, the editor of the controversial *Sonntagsblatt*. Schubert's fascination with Schiller's texts, beginning in 1811, can only be compared with his profound admiration of Goethe's poetry, a sudden revelation in the fall of 1814. Schubert's very first setting of a text from Goethe's *Faust* turned out to be an undisputed masterwork: *Gretchen am Spinnrade*, D.118.

It is not clear why Schubert was so late in finding his way to Goethe, by way of Schiller and Matthisson. (During this period he made a few settings of texts by Metastasio, Rochlitz, Hölty, and Herder.) Friedrich von Gentz, politician, scholar, and journalist, arrived in Vienna in 1808, shortly after Metternich had authorized new editions of the classic writers. Gentz believed that "no young Viennese girl of 17 or 18 had any excuse for not knowing

Goethe's works reasonably well."[9] In 1811 Schubert, though not yet 17, seems to have begun composing songs that presupposed some acquaintance with literature. But he dared not for some time approach Goethe who, thanks to Schlegel's activity, was even more esteemed by the educated Viennese than Schiller. Such respect for the great man was fortunately not an obstacle to coming to terms with his work; nor did it cause him to write uninspired settings in the style of Zelter, a posture which Schubert's friends may have helped him in adopting. Josef von Spaun in particular may have acted as Schubert's mentor at this time, as well as in 1816 when he approached Goethe on Schubert's behalf. After all, it was Spaun who had earlier put Schubert in touch with Theodor Körner and who in 1814 had introduced Schubert to Johann Mayrhofer and, shortly thereafter Franz von Schober.

Körner's *Zriny* had been a success in the 1812 season. He held the appointment of "Imperial Theater Poet." His predecessor in that position (a title sure to impress all lovers of the theater) had been no other than Kotzebue. Körner's appearance was not impressive, but thanks to his ardent patriotism and his affair with the popular actress Antonie Adamberger he was the subject of much conversation. As a poet he was clearly indebted to Schiller. Schubert may not have been acquainted with Körner's poetry during the poet's lifetime, but when in 1814 Körner's father published the volume of poems entitled *Leyer und Schwert*, Schubert composed some of them.

With the settings of Mayrhofer a period of song writing began in which Schubert chose poems penned not only by the great classic writers but also by his friends, among them Josef Kenner, Schober, Franz X. Schlechta, Albert Stadler, Spaun, Heinrich Hüttenbrenner, Bruchmann, and Kupelwieser. In some instances Schubert may have set poems purely as an expression of friendship. Often these songs are merely sprinkled among other works.

Mayrhofer was an exception. Ludwig August Frankl describes him as a shy, timid person.[10] As a sensitive, music-loving student he won Schubert's friendship which seems to have become closer in the fall of 1816 since the number of songs on Mayrhofer's texts increased greatly thereafter. Mayrhofer wrote in a powerful Romantic language which may have had an effect on Schubert's general way of thinking, for at this very time he began keeping a diary which dealt with poetry and philosophy, rather than merely recording events. Mayrhofer's influence disappeared after 1820 when he was appointed *Bücherrevisor* (examiner of books), i.e., a censor. There may be a good reason why Schubert's name is not found in the list of subscribers for the volume of Mayrhofer's poetry published in 1824 by Friedrich Volke in Vienna.

Schubert's literary sources were greatly varied, representing many poetic currents, which tells us something about his interests and education. Such evidence should lead us to a conclusion that is at variance with the commonly held opinion that Schubert's general education was inadequate. Schubert was an artist who held liberal views, who knew his way through the intellectual currents of the time and whose creative work was stimulated by them. His familiarity with classical literature explains his preference for Goethe and Schiller, with an occasional bow to Matthisson.

If Austrian poetry does not figure prominently in the body of Schubert's work, one must remember that in the early 1800s there hardly were any major Austrian poets. Grillparzer, deeply rooted in the rationalistic ideas of Josephinism, was considered the great hope of Austrian literature, yet he was neither very popular nor did his works receive critical scrutiny for some years. He was a government official which made him suspect among the literati. Grillparzer was both hurt and annoyed by this reception and especially by the controversy carried on in the press relative to the "tragic" qualities of his *Ahnfrau.*[11] Schubert made Grillparzer's acquaintance at the time of this debate, and Grillparzer requested him to compose *Bertas Lied in der Nacht* (Bertha's Lullaby), D.653, for use in later performances of *Die Ahnfrau.* In all, Grillparzer's poetry does not seem to have struck Schubert as the kind that cries for music for he set surprisingly few of his texts.

Though Schubert preferred setting poetry by the classic writers, among whose texts he ranged widely, he never looked exclusively to a single author. For example, in his "year of songs," (1815) he composed songs on texts by Goethe but also by Friedrich Anton Bertrand, Ludwig Hölty, James Macpherson, Josef Kenner, and Ludwig Kosegarten. Whether a poem was considered romantic or "reactionary" was of no interest to him; his only concern was limited to its suitability for music. Knowing the diverse quarters in which he sought inspiration assists us in forming an idea of the literature which was in vogue in Vienna at the time. Certain trends are clearly recognizable, though Schubert also turned to older poetry that reappeared in new editions. Kosegarten and Hölty belong here, along with Klopstock and his "sublime" poetry. These poets figure importantly in the 1815 songs but he seldom returned to them in later years, even though Bernhard Philipp Bauer, a respected Viennese publisher, reissued the poetry of all three. Beginning in 1816 Schubert turned to texts by August Wilhelm and Friedrich Schlegel, as well as Johann Gaudenz von Salis-Seewis whose lyrics are modeled on those of Matthisson and

Hölty. It seems significant that their poetry was published at about the same time by the above-mentioned Bauer.

Austria's literary scene changed markedly after 1820. Schlegel, living in retirement in Vienna, had turned his attention to the philosophy of history as well as politics and sociology. He articulated a decidedly Christian point of view, which shows that the Catholic restauration was progressing in Austria. Truly significant literary contributions were made only by Raimund and Grillparzer. The latter continually ran afoul of the censors who became increasingly strict after 1819. When his *König Ottokars Glück und Ende* (King Ottokar's Good Fortune and Death) was banned in 1824, he was so enraged that he threatened to emigrate.[12] But his light fiction and poetry written for special occasions continued to flourish despite these restrictions. Almanacs and periodicals provided the vehicle for the publication of sentimental stories, usually in installments. Some journals were devoted to more substantial literary fare and to the dissemination of news, including the *Wiener Zeitschrift für Kunst, Literatur, Theater und Mode* (The Vienna Journal of Art, Literature, Theater and Fashion) which included occasional music supplements in which several Schubert songs were first published. As always serious literature appealed to only a small audience, so the practice of presenting readings in an intimate social setting was adopted. In addition the appearance of "pocket book" editions provided a convenient vehicle for presenting plays in parts, to be read in such settings.

One such "reading society" developed within the Schubert circle; formed in the early 1820s through the initiative of Franz von Schober, an actor who had been Schubert's friend since 1815 and in whose apartment the group met. When Schober left for Breslau late in 1823, the reading society met in the quarters of the painter Ludwig

Mohn. Schubert took part in Schober's gatherings while he lived in the actor's apartment in the Göttweiger Hof from 1822–23. Later, frictions arose between members of the circle and the readings were discontinued in the spring of 1824. In November 1823 Schubert reported the unpleasant atmosphere at the meetings to Schober:

> Our reading society is in sad shape. As I predicted, it lost its focus when you left. We admitted four new members to replace you and Kupelwieser . . . but they are very ordinary students and civil servants. Whenever Bruchmann is absent, Mohn takes charge, and all he talks about are horses and hounds, riding and fencing. If things continue like this I shan't be able to stand their company much longer.[13]

Quite evidently Schubert had little in common with a group devoid of artistic interests.

We know little of the literary tastes of this circle, save that they read Goethe's *Torquato Tasso.* Following Schober's return to Vienna he became the central figure in another circle which read works by Kleist, Heinrich Heine, and Ludwig Tieck.[14] In 1826 they chose to read Heine's *Reisebilder,* which inspired Schubert to select and compose six poems from its first section, the cycle *Heimkehr* (The Homecoming) which were eventually included in the group of songs published posthumously as *Schwanengesang* (Swan Song), D.957. Unquestionably, Schubert the composer was stimulated by this literary environment.

It also appears that while Spaun was Schubert's mentor in the composer's student years and again later, Schober served that purpose during the 1820s. Schober, a man of the world, has been accused of having exerted a "bad" influence on Schubert, yet there were good reasons why Schubert counted him among his closest friends, receiving much stimulation from him. A well educated man, Schober could evaluate critically Vienna's stagnating literary life. His taste had been refined and broadened by travel; he was one of the few among Schubert's friends and acquaintances who had lived abroad for extended periods. He must have noted the freer intellectual climate in Germany, uninhibited by censorship. This stimulating environment was manifest in the "Young Germany" movement which advocated an entirely new view of the social role of literature, which grew out of a reaction to the Goethe period and subscribed to a most radical form of liberalism. Schober was thus able to relate to the Schubert circle invaluable insights on the German literary scene. All of this may bear some relation to the fact that Goethe's texts no longer figure prominently among Schubert's songs in the last years of the composer's life.

That Schober provided his friend Schubert with the poems by Wilhelm Müller, though conjecture, is at least a possibility. It is quite likely that Schubert's introduction to Müller's poems came about through Carl Maria von Weber who knew the poet.[15]

Müller had written his cycle of poems, *Die schöne Müllerin* (The Beautiful Maid of the Mill), as a *Liederspiel* (Song Play) for friends in Berlin who included artists and writers. He later revised the cycle which appeared in 1821 as part of a collection entitled *Sieben und siebzig Gedichte aus den hinterlassenen Papieren eines reisenden Waldhornisten* (Seventy-seven Poems From the Papers Left By a Traveling Horn Player). Several Berlin composers, among them Ludwig Berger and Bernhard Josef Klein, soon set them to music, but today their settings are little more than historical curiosities. Among his contemporaries Müller was regarded as a lover of ancient Greece, having written a very well received collection of poems entitled *Lieder der Griechen* (Songs of Greece). He may also be remembered by some for his drinking songs which found their way into

German student song books. It is unlikely that Müller's name was known among Vienna's literati, which makes plausible the assumption that someone must have specifically called Schubert's attention to him, thus inspiring the composition of *Die schöne Müllerin*, D.795, and, later, *Winterreise* (Winter Journey), D.911.

In the Vienna of the 1820s there were other literary currents that stimulated Schubert's song writing, among which were the works of the Scotch writer Walter Scott. By 1815 his historical novels had attracted a large following in Germany where they retained their popularity for more than 20 years. It took a little longer in Vienna: his works did not appear there until 1825, in several editions, heralded by a "publicity campaign" in the press that was unheard of at the time they appeared. Scott quickly became the object of widespread veneration. The singer Johann Michael Vogl declared Scott to be his favorite author, while Caroline Pichler demonstrated her enthusiasm by translating *Lady of the Lake*. In 1825 Schubert composed seven poems from that work, but used a translation by Adam Storck, a professor of German literature who had died in Bremen in 1822. The date of Schubert's composition, together with a letter of August 1823 to Schober, in which he mentions that he was then reading Scott,[16] indicates that he knew some of Scott's work before the writer became generally known in Vienna's literary circles.

It is not widely appreciated that Schubert typically evaluated and chose his texts with great care, nor that his assessments were often penned with biting scorn. At the time he occupied himself with Scott he gave to Spaun this interesting description of the literary situation in Vienna: "The bland, ossified prose with which we are inundated these days is indeed miserable, all the more so since people seem to be quite comfortable with it while they slowly sink farther and farther into the morass."[17]

Schubert's level of literacy as a composer or performer at the time was remarkably high, though it is hard for us today to retrace all his literary encounters. Since he frequently changed living quarters, he owned few books, as witnessed by the small library he left in Schober's hands after his death. Indeed a careful examination of his oeuvre justifies a different view of his place in contemporary intellectual and cultural life than the commonly accepted one which is based on remarks by sundry contemporaries.

Schubert testifies to the very high intellectual level of some circles in the Biedermeier era in Vienna. He was by no means one who followed the crowd during an epoch that has unfairly been accused of a hostile attitude to foreign cultural influences. It will take some time before devotees become used to the image of Schubert as a man of many interests. Future writers on Schubert might therefore heed the assessment made in 1825 by Anton Ottenwald:

> Schubert was so friendly, so communicative . . . I never knew him to be other than serious, profound, enthusiastic. He talked in the same way about art, poetry, his youth, his friends and other influential people in his life, and about the relation of ideas to life. I never ceased to be impressed by his mind; yet people claimed that his composing was instinctive—that he hardly knew or understood what he was doing, or how; it all seemed so simple. I cannot talk about the entire range of his beliefs, but they reveal insights that go beyond anything appropriated from others. Good friends may have had a part in this, but this in no way diminishes his originality.[18]

The Composer in His Time

"You lucky fellow; I really envy you! You live a life of sweet, precious freedom, can give free rein to your musical genius, can express your thoughts in any way you like—are loved, admired, and praised to the sky!"[1]

Schubert's brother Ignaz wrote these lines to Franz in 1818. Ignaz, heavily burdened by teaching duties and resentful of his "stupid superiors," paints an unrealistically rosy picture of his brother's life who by then was unemployed, having left his position as an assistant teacher. In a way, Schubert achieved Beethoven's aim: to free the artist from dependence upon the generosity of the aristocracy. But this accomplishment brought with it problems that were virtually insoluble. Much talk about the "democratization"[2] of art did not pay his living expenses.

It is true that Schubert repeatedly applied for public appointments, supported by recommendations of various friends or well wishers. He applied for the positions of music teacher in Laibach and Vice-Kapellmeister at the Austrian court in Vienna. He may also have felt qualified to assume the post of vocal coach at the Kärntnertortheater. One gains the impression, however, that all these applications were made half-heartedly and largely at the instigation of friends. Just why in each case other applicants were preferred can no longer be established. To say that he was little known at the time is invalidated by the number of known performances of his works. Schubert must have displayed some personal qualities that led others to see him as unsuited for such official positions. The reports which have come down to us differ greatly and in some cases are contradictory. He was said to be uneducated (an unjust assertion dealt with in the preceding chapter), to have a "brusk"[3] manner, to be "frivolous and unreliable,"[4] but was also praised for his "open, sincere way of thinking."[5] Schubert himself sought the explanation in his own personality as is evidenced by a valuable letter to a Frau Pachler in Graz.

> I now realize just how well off I was in Grätz, for I cannot get used to Vienna. It's such a big city, and one misses people who are cordial and sincere, who think worth-while thoughts, who have sensible things to say and inspired things to do. People chatter so much; it makes me wonder whether I am smart or dumb. It's hard to feel truly happy here. It is possible, of course, that I am to blame, for it takes me a long time to warm up to such people.[6]

Schubert here hints at his own introverted nature; it may explain the indecisiveness with which he pursued goals that might have been advantageous for an artist. He was reluctant to push himself. This quotation is also signifi-cant in the unfavorable impression it conveys of his circle of Viennese friends. It seems to confirm what I pointed out in an earlier chapter dealing with the Schubertiads.

Generally speaking, Schubert was not up to holding his own amongst the manifold, elaborate intrigues which characterized Vienna's musical scene even then. Even the Gesellschaft der Musikfreunde was not above intrigues. When in 1818 he applied for membership as an "active" musician, he was rejected without any stated reason.[7] Yet at almost the same time the Gesellschaft, in a public statement, referred to his compositions as "masterworks."[8]

Schubert's first official honors were bestowed on him in 1823—not in Vienna, but in Graz and Linz, by the most significant supporters of music in those cities, the music societies. His first recognition in Vienna, by the Gesellschaft der Musikfreunde, did not come until 1825, and then at a private meeting, which may well explain why this fact has remained unknown until only recently.[9] Schubert was elected as an alternate on the governing board of the Gesellschaft, which placed him in the company of well-known musical figures, among them Assmayr, Castelli, Aloys Fuchs, Tobias Haslinger, Georg Rafael Kiesewetter, and Sonnleithner. Two years later he was advanced to the ranks of a "regular" member.

The recognition which he did not receive as a person in public music life was accorded his music. To the surprise of modern Schubert scholars this recognition came rather early. It seems that Schubert's talent as a composer was recognized by those with a special interest in the arts while he was still quite young and virtually unknown in public. It is to the credit of the Gesellschaft der Musikfreunde, which in Schubert's case did not display prophetic gifts, that the connoisseurs belonged to its ranks. In March 1818 Schubert's Overture D.591 was performed at a concert given by Jaëll and shortly thereafter at another private musical occasion. The same spring the Gesellschaft announced a series of musical *Abendunterhaltungen* (Evening Entertainments), mentioning Schubert as one of the most significant composers of the time. The announcement pointed out that "with the participation of such excellent musicians" the Gesellschaft could "properly perform the masterworks of a Haydn, Mozart, Beethoven, Onslow, Spohr, Schubert and others."[10] In the event the Gesellschaft was unable to make good on these promises, but five years later on another occasion Schubert's name figured with those of the musical luminaries of the day—an occasion which, significantly, did not take place in Vienna. In the spring of 1825 Giovanni Ricordi, the Italian music publisher whose firm in Milan was already well established, announced a *Biblioteca di musica moderna* (Library of Modern Music) in which Schubert is included in the company of Beethoven, Clementi, Rossini and others.[11]

Performances of Schubert's stage works, given at the Kärntnertortheater and the Theater an der Wien, were merely reported in the press as news items. The first recognition of Schubert as a truly talented composer occurred in other German-speaking countries. The *Abendzeitung* in Dresden of January 30, 1821 included a story, written by a Viennese, to be sure, that

> Schubert, a young composer, has written several songs by the best poets, notably Goethe. They display profound knowledge coupled with admirable talent, and are attracting the attention of connoisseurs. He knows how to paint with music; his songs *Die Forelle*, *Gretchen am Spinnrad* (Faust), and *Der Kampf* (Schiller) are so convincing and realistic that they surpass anything previously created in the genre of the Lied. To my knowledge they have not yet been engraved but are circulated only in manuscript copies.[12]

The *Allgemeine Musikalische Zeitung* in Vienna required a year to devote a long article to his songs which by that time had been issued in separate collections beginning in April 1821. The reviewer, apparently a member of the Schubert circle, used the publication of the Op. 7 Lieder as the occasion to "call attention to the works of this eminent talent," and, by doing this, to "render a welcome service to all devotees of truly expressive song."[13] The review appeared rather late, at a time when the first song collections had gained significant sales. They had been issued, in an unusually large printing, by Cappi & Diabelli, but as many of Schubert's friends bought copies they soon were out of print.

Schubert, the composer of songs, had suddenly stepped into the limelight and so was adopted by the arrangers of private recitals and the music journals. Soon after the article in the *Allgemeine Musikalische Zeitung* another appeared in the *Wiener Zeitschrift für Kunst, Literatur, Theater und Mode*[14]. Its author, Friedrich von Hentl, was an alumnus of the *Theresianische Ritterakademie* whose acquaintance Schubert had probably made at a concert in honor of the Emperor's birthday. Hentl's essay, *Blick auf Schuberts Lieder* (A Look at Schubert's Songs) is quite detailed and clearly articulates the author's favorable opinion. He displayed considerable musical knowledge and an eagerness to emphasize the significance of Schubert's works to a public not celebrated for refined taste. "Schubert's Lieder without a doubt have the qualities that place them among the greatest, most inspired masterworks. Thus they can serve to raise taste from its present low level. ... German music must be congratulated for harboring such a genius. Thanks to his remarkable talents he has again and again given musical meaning to the masterworks of German poetry." Other "experts" now eagerly joined the ranks in praise of Schubert's songs. Again it is worth noting that the foreign press, in Berlin, Munich, Frankfurt and Dresden, devoted much more space to this new genre than the Viennese journals. We need not doubt that these reviewers were quite sincerely impressed by Schubert's "musical poems", a term coined by C. A. Spina, Diabelli's successor. Their insistent praise was undoubtedly a response to the lack of earlier major Lieder composers. Since the songs of Mozart and Beethoven were, with the exception of Beethoven's *Adelaide*, virtually forgotten, writers could endorse Schubert's place without reservation.

The reception of Schubert's instrumental works was another matter. During his lifetime publishers showed little interest in them save for his dance music. His instrumental music was not widely known even though reviewers tended to compare it with that of Beethoven, Haydn, or even Cramer. Schubert's piano works were greatly esteemed abroad, but not in the city of his birth. Hans Georg Nägeli, a Swiss composer and music teacher, founded a music publishing firm in Zürich in 1791. Beginning in 1826 his "Lectures on Music" listed "contemporary composers for the pianoforte ... whose imaginative music enriches the art of our time" and included Czerny, Kalkbrenner, Neukomm—and Schubert.[15] Nägeli also intended to list Schubert in his *Musikalische Ehrenpforte* (Musical Hall of Honor) but for unknown reasons this plan was not carried through. Schubert's Piano Sonata in A Minor, Op. 42, D.845, published by Pennauer in Vienna in 1826, especially impressed Nägeli; he referred to its first movement as "a capital piece."[16] The sonata was first reviewed in the *Allgemeine Musikalische Zeitung* in Leipzig, the first known critique of a major instrumental work by Schubert. The reviewer, not well acquainted with Vienna's musical life, wrote that "especially in Northern Germany Schubert is known only by his songs for one or more voices, with or without piano accompaniment, all of them showing great variety."[17] He pointed to the future when he remarked that "having examined Schubert's songs, their good points and their shortcomings," he predicts "he would be even more successful in instrumental music, especially in its freer and larger forms. The present work, his first large sonata, completely confirms this belief."

One looks in vain for such perceptive reviews in the Viennese papers. In the case of the Op. 42 sonata another year was to pass before the editor of the *Wiener Zeitschrift für Kunst, Literatur, Theater und Mode* condescended to introduce the work with the schoolmasterly note that "the entire sonata . . . offers many opportunities to the thoughtful player to show his interpretive skills."[18]

In general Schubert was not blessed with perceptive reviewers of his instrumental music. Even Rochlitz, well-trained musically, who had been quick to recognize Beethoven's genius, seemed helpless when dealing with Schubert, writing that "this talented artist only needs a knowledgeable friend who would enlighten him in a spirit of love, telling him what he is, what he can do, and wants. From this, we hope, he would discover on his own what he should do."[19] No doubt Rochlitz's remarks were well-intended advice; they represent the typical, insecure attempts of his contemporaries where Schubert's instrumental music was concerned.

Evidently neither critics nor audiences could imagine that, in the same period and immediately following Beethoven, other composers could write instrumental music of artistic stature. One observer even saw "dangers" in such a succession, commenting that it seemed inconceivable and inadmissible that another could "begin where a great master, who so significantly and daringly extended the boundaries of his art, had left off."[20] Though he was always given credit for talent contemporaries did not expect Schubert to produce any instrumental music that went beyond being "creditable."[21] It seemed easier to find such a slot for him than to come to terms with a composer of Beethoven's stature. Even during the last year of his life, and after his private concert during which some of his chamber music was played, no change in public opinion can be detected. A Vienna review of his *Rondeau brillant pour Pianoforte et Violin*, D.895, which had been published by Artaria in 1827, again praises his "magnificent talent" and imaginative treatment of the musical material but referred to him as the "well-known composer of Lieder and Romanzen,"[22] which is certainly a case of damning his instrumental works with faint praise. One might attempt to offset this shallow appraisal by noting the excellent review, in the same issue of the *Wiener Zeitschrift,* of the first part of *Winterreise,* which had been published by Haslinger early in 1828. But such a facile trade-off only distorts the true state of affairs: during his lifetime Schubert was considered *the* Lieder composer without equal, so his success in this genre was bound to overshadow all of his other musical accomplishments.

Nor did his sacred music find any significant recognition. To succeed, Schubert would have had to pit himself against such musical "princes of the church" as Seyfried, Preindl, Eybler and others. This competition alone may have kept Schubert from undertaking the effort. Only one of his Masses was printed: the Mass in C Major, D.452, of 1816, and even this was probably attributable to the efforts of Michael Holzer, former choirmaster of the Lichtenthal Church, to whom the work is dedicated.

To the question of whether Schubert was popular in his own time one can only answer that he was known and appreciated in certain circles. He was not "popular" in the sense of having his name appear frequently in the daily papers or fashionable journals. He displayed no talent for promoting himself in a way that might have insured popular success. To do so he would have had to pursue a showman's style such as Schober once described to him, a style of self-promotion still effective today: "These dogs have no feelings or thoughts of their own; they respond to noise and to the opinions of others. If only you could find a few critics who would noisily beat your drum you'd surely succeed. I know some very insignificant people who achieved fame and popularity in that way."[23]

In this sense Beethoven was not popular either, but well known and esteemed. He was already a legend in his lifetime; music lovers and critics alike, voicing their opinions in musical journals, considered him among the greatest of artists, along with Mozart and Haydn. For the much younger Schubert the road to recognition was long and arduous. He was no doubt intensely aware of the strong artistic pressure which Beethoven, unintentionally, exerted on the city's musical life. Schubert was one of those who clearly understood and appreciated the high standards established by Beethoven. Quite evidently he was self-conscious and hesitant when it came to composing in genres for which Beethoven had created the models for some years to come. For all serious composers of the age, Beethoven's instrumental works represented a body of music that was extraordinarily difficult to comprehend yet intensely fascinating. Schubert was bound to understand that these works, especially those written after 1814, not only influenced his own composing but also formed an obstacle to his own artistic growth. In short, Beethoven's music was to be the yardstick by which Schubert's music, too, was measured, and not by its unique and distinctive qualities.

The years after 1814 were witness to the crisis in Schubert's development as a composer. The period from 1817 to 1824 was especially difficult. Beethoven's 7th, 8th, and 9th symphonies appeared then (Schubert attended Beethoven's concert in May 1824 which featured the Ninth Symphony and parts of the *Missa Solemnis*), as well as the Piano Sonatas Op. 90, 101, 106, 109 and 110; the String Quartet Op. 95, the String Quintet Op. 104, and the Diabelli Variations Op. 120. Editions of these compositions had been published by Steiner & Co. and by Artaria, and were readily available in Vienna.

Schubert struggled mightily to define his own musical style, especially its formal aspects, as he worked in genres in which Beethoven had made major developmental changes. By way of example: before 1816 Schubert

wrote in rapid succession several conventionally conceived string quartets. Following this outpouring artistic
reservations apparently restrained him from further work
in this manner. From 1817 until 1824, when he returned to
quartet writing, we have only one complete movement for
a quartet, D.703. By the age of 20 Schubert had written six
symphonies; but only then did he begin to come to terms
in earnest with problems of symphonic style. His experi-
ments after 1818, evidently made under Beethoven's
influence, he referred to as "the road to the great symphony."[24] Several symphonic fragments fell by the
roadside, but a milestone was reached when in the spring
of 1825 he began composing the "Great" Symphony in C
Major, D.944.[25] Thoughts of further symphonies occupied
him until shortly before his death. Had these sketches
been fashioned into a complete work[26] Schubert would
surely have paved the way for the development of the
symphonic form which was not realized until the late 19th
century.

Around 1815 Schubert began to seriously occupy
himself with the piano sonata; by 1817 he had written
several. A number of sonatas written in and after 1818
remained incomplete; the period of his great piano sonatas
was delayed until 1825 beginning with the Sonata Op. 42,
D.845. Its appearance marked the end of the "crisis" that
had characterized his instrumental writing for the pre-
vious 11 years.

Schubert's "last period" opens with the String
Quartet in A Minor, Op. 29, D.804. This late work appeared
at the same time as Beethoven's last works. While
Beethoven was able to attend to the publishing of his late
quartets, discussing them with the publisher, Schubert
could only make offers to publishers, chiefly abroad. The
public therefore knew next to nothing of his last works and
so could form no opinion of their artistic value.

112

To argue that if one *had* known them one would have been reluctant to compare them with Beethoven amounts to drawing conclusions based on incorrect premises. Nor can we use statistics alone to establish the degree to which Schubert was known and appreciated, as did the catalogue of the 1978 Schubert exhibition at the *Gesellschaft der Musikfreunde* in which we read that "during a period of eight years 106 works (opus numbers) by Schubert appeared in print, whereas during 32 years only 30 more works by Beethoven were published, excluding those that appeared without opus numbers. The latter, however, are more numerous in Schubert's case."[27] Using such statistics the author intended to prove that Schubert received roughly as much recognition during his lifetime as did Beethoven. These calculations ignore the fact that the works cited (certainly a significant number) consist largely of Lieder and dance music, but do not include, as in Beethoven's case, any symphonies, only one string quartet (D.804), one Mass (D.452) and, among Schubert's many piano sonatas, only three from 1825/26 (D.845, 850, 894). Only many years later did posterity "discover" his String Quintet, D.956, the *Arpeggione* Sonata, D.821, the great Octet, D.803, and the C Major Symphony, D.944. So statistics used out of context only distort the facts if the weight and significance of individual opus numbers are not taken into account.

Certainly, Schubert was not unknown in his day. In 1825 Cappi & Co. announced "an extremely good portrait of the composer."[28] And among those who looked for more than a "feast for the ears"[29], as the singer Anna Milder put it, interest in his music gradually grew. This, at any rate, was the trend, though his contemporaries may not have had a clear idea about his place in the musical and intellectual life of the time.

Later generations were fond of viewing Schubert as

the artist who lived in and represented the Biedermeier age, but his major works, whether vocal or instrumental, are in no way representative of that age. Like Beethoven, Schubert is quite atypical of the Biedermeier, even though he readily made concessions to what that age required, including the composition of dance music. Actually (as we pointed out in our chapter on literature[30]), a contrary view seems correct: without Beethoven, Schubert, Grillparzer or Raimund, Austria's intellectual life during the Biedermeier would have been impoverished. From today's perspective we can add that in terms of impact on the artistic world in general, Beethoven and Schubert are the only figures of significance. Both gave to the period its characteristic imprint; Beethoven for more than two decades, Schubert for barely one. We can further distinguish between the two by recalling that Schubert was the true representative of Vienna's cultural life. While Beethoven found an adopted home in Vienna, Schubert was born and lived there, becoming one of the city's most eminent sons.

Chronology

1763   Franz Theodor Schubert (father) born in Neudorf in Moravia.

1770   Birth of Beethoven and Hölderlin.

1784   Schubert's father appointed "school assistant" in Vienna—Leopoldstadt. Birth of Louis Spohr.

1785   Schubert's father moves to Vienna—Lichtenthal; marries Elizabeth Vietz.

1786   Birth of Carl Maria v. Weber.

1791   Death of Mozart. Birth of Grillparzer.

1792   Beginning of the first War of the Coalition; birth of Rossini.

1793   Birth of the painter Ferdinand Waldmüller.

1794   Birth of Ferdinand Schubert.

1795   First performance of a work by Beethoven at a concert of the *Tonkünstler-Societät* in Vienna.

1796   Composition of Beethoven's *Adelaide* and of K. F. Zelter's first collection of songs. J. R. Zumsteeg writes his *Twelve Songs*.

1797   Birth of Franz Peter Schubert. Austria threatened by Napoleon Bonaparte. Birth of Heinrich Heine. Goethe's *Hermann und Dorothea*. Joseph Haydn composes his *Emperor Hymn*. Beethoven's Quintet, Op. 26 first performed. Birth of Gaetano Donizetti.

1798   J. F. Rochlitz founds the *Allgemeine musikalische Zeitung* in Leipzig. First performance of Haydn's *Seven Last Words* at a concert of the *Tonkünstler-Societät*.

1799   Napoleon's coup d'etat. Beginning of 2nd War of the Coalition. Birth of Balzac and Pushkin. Schiller's *Wallenstein* and *Lied von der Glocke*. Birth of Halévy. Beethoven completes the *Pathétique Sonata*, Op. 13. First performance of Haydn's *Creation*.

1800   Schiller completes *Maria Stuart*. Beethoven's First Symphony, Third Piano Concerto and String Quartets Op. 18. Cherubini's opera *Les deux journées*; Zumsteeg, *Lieder und Balladen*. Beethoven gives his first concert at the Kärntnertortheater; Prince Lichnowsky grants him a yearly salary.

1801   The Schubert family moves to the Säulengasse. Opening of the Theater an der Wien with Schikaneder's *Thespis Traum*. Birth of Bellini, Josef Lanner, Albert Lortzing. Beethoven's letter to the "Immortal Beloved." First performance of Haydn's *The Seasons* by the *Tonkünstler-Societät*.

1802   Birth of Lenau, Victor Hugo, Alexandre Dumas, Sr. Beethoven's "Heiligenstadt Testament."

1803   The *Stadtkonvikt* founded by Emperor Francis. Death of Herder and Klopstock. Birth of Berlioz.

1804   Napoleon proclaimed emperor; Emperor Francis assumes the title of hereditary Emperor of Austria. Death of Kant; birth of Mörike. Schiller writes *William Tell*. Birth of Moritz v. Schwind and Johann Strauss, Sr. Beethoven completes the *Eroica*

Symphony; it has its first (private) performance by the orchestra of Prince Lobkowitz.

1805   Third War of the Coalition. Napoleon conquers Austria and resides at Schönbrunn Castle. Birth of Adalbert Stifter, Hans Christian Andersen. Death of Schiller. Birth of Boccherini. First performance of Beethoven's *Fidelio* at the Theater an der Wien.

1806   First performance of Beethoven's Violin Concerto and *Leonore Overture,* No. 3 and of Cherubini's opera *Faniska* at the Kärntnertortheater.

1807   Schubert is introduced to Salieri and may have become his private pupil. Founding of the *Liebhaberkonzerte.* Beethoven writes his *Mass in C;* first performance of his Fourth Symphony. First performance of Spontini's opera *La vestale* in Paris.

1808   Schubert becomes a choir boy at the Hofkapelle and enters the Stadtkonvikt. Publication of Goethe's *Faust,* Part I. Friedrich Gentz, Clemens Maria Hofbauer and Friedrich v. Schlegel reside in Vienna. August Wilhelm v. Schlegel's "Lectures on Dramatic Art and Literature" in Vienna. Gala performance of Haydn's *Creation* in the Great Hall of the University; first performances of Beethoven's Fifth and Sixth Symphonies. Performance of Gluck's *Armida* at the Theater an der Wien.

1809   A memorandum of the Stadtkonvikt for the first time refers to Schubert as "a musical talent." Austria's insurrection against Napoleon fails; Metternich becomes Foreign Minister. Death of Haydn. Birth of Mendelssohn. K. F. Zelter founds the Berlin *Liedertafel.*

1810   Schubert writes his *Fantasy in G*, D.1, his first dated composition. Marriage of Napoleon and Marie Louise. Invention of rapid printing press for books. Works by Goethe, Schiller, and Kotzebue begin to appear in Vienna. F. v. Schlegel founds and edits the *Österreichischer Beobachter*. Birth of Schumann, Chopin, Otto Nicolai. Review of Beethoven's Fifth Symphony by E. T. A. Hoffmann. Performance of Gluck's *Iphigénie en Tauride* at the Theater an der Wien.

1811   Schubert receives thorough-bass lessons from Wenzel Ruzicka. First attempts at composing symphonic and stage works; first Lied, *Hagars Klage*, D.5; first setting of a Schiller text, *Leichenfantasie*, D.7. Goethe's *Dichtung und Wahrheit*. Eichendorff completes his studies in Vienna. Theodor Körner moves to Vienna. Birth of Liszt and Ambroise Thomas.

1812   Schubert's voice changes: he loses his place as a choir boy; studies counterpoint with Salieri. He composes sections of Masses and string quartets. Death of Schubert's mother. The Grimm Brothers publish their collection of fairy tales, *Kinder-und Hausmärchen*. F. Schlegel lectures on "Old and New German Literature" in Vienna. Körner's *Zriny* first performed at the Theater an der Wien. Beethoven meets Goethe at Teplitz. Gala opening of the theater in Pest with Beethoven's *König Stephan*. Founding of the Gesellschaft der Musikfreunde in Vienna.

1813   Schubert leaves the Stadtkonvikt and attends the *Lehrerbildungsanstalt* (Normal School); he completes his First Symphony, D.82, begins the opera *Des Teufels Lustschloss*, D.84, and composes songs and quartets. Schubert's father marries Anna Kleyenböck. The Battle of the Nations at Leipzig; Wellington's victory at Vittoria. Birth of Kierkegaard, Friedrich Hebbel, Georg Büchner. Körner is killed in the battle of Gadebusch. Clemens v. Brentano comes to Vienna; M. v. Collin becomes censor. Birth of Wagner and Verdi. Spohr becomes director of the orchestra at the Theater an der Wien. First performances of Beethoven's Seventh Symphony; first performances of Rossini's *Tancredi* and *L'Italiana in Algeri* in Venice. Weber's *Abu Hassan* given at the Theater an der Wien.

1814 Schubert makes the acquaintance of Johann Mayrhofer. Performance of his Mass in F Major, D.105 in Lichtenthal and in the Augustinerkirche under his direction. *Gretchen am Spinnrade*, D.118, his first important Lied. Completion of his opera *Des Teufels Lustschloss*, D.84. He begins work on his Second Symphony, D.125. Abdication of Napoleon; Peace Treaty of Paris, beginning of the Congress of Vienna. The preacher Zacharias Werner moves to Vienna. Beethoven arranges two concerts in the Redoutensaal; the third version of his *Fidelio* is performed in the presence of the monarchs attending the Congress.

1815 Schubert composes over 100 songs, the Mass in G Major, D.167, and the stage works *Der vierjährige Posten*, D.190, *Fernando*, D.220, and *Claudine von Villa Bella*, D.239. Completion of the Third Symphony D.200 and first attempts at piano sonatas. Beginning of Schubert's friendship with Franz v. Schober. End of the Congress of Vienna; restoration of the Church State. Austria joins the Holy Alliance. Birth of Bismarck. First performance of Z. Werner's *Der Wahn* at the Vienna Burgtheater. Birth of Robert Franz. Mälzel invents the metronome. Beethoven is granted Viennese citizenship, without payment of taxes. First *Gesellschaftskonzert* of the Gesellschaft der Musikfreunde in Vienna.

1816   Schubert applies unsuccessfully for the position of music teacher in Laibach. J. Spaun unsuccessfully writes to Goethe on Schubert's behalf. Schubert begins to keep a diary. Performance of his Second Symphony by a Viennese orchestral association. Composition of his Fourth Symphony, D.417. He writes over 100 songs; among the poets are Goethe, Matthisson, Schober, Fouqué, Schiller, Ossian, Klopstock, Schlegel, Hölty, Uz, and Mayrhofer. Bernhard Philip Bauer in Vienna reprints works by Kosegarten, Hölty and Klopstock, also texts by A. W. and F. Schlegel, Salis-Seewis and others. Rossini completes the *Barber of Seville;* his *Tancredi* is first given at the Kärntnertortheater.

1817   Schubert is introduced to the singer Johann Michael Vogl. The Schubert family moves to the Rossau where his father obtains a teaching position. *The Trout,* D.550, and the first piano sonatas are written; work on the Sixth Symphony begins. Performance of the overture "In the Italian Style," D.591. First mention of Schubert's name in a journal, the *Wiener Allgemeine Theaterzeitung.* Count Josef Sedlnitzky becomes chief of police and aide to Metternich. First performance of Grillparzer's *Ahnfrau* at the Theater an der Wien. Ferdinand Raimund joins the Theater in der Leopoldstadt. Founding of the conservatory of the Gesellschaft der Musikfreunde. The *Allgemeine musikalische Zeitung* begins publication in Vienna. Beethoven directs his Eighth Symphony in the Redoutensaal. Rossini's *Tancredi* and *Ciro in Babilonia* given at the Theater an der Wien.

1818   Schubert distances himself from his family and becomes a freelance musician; he tries in vain to become an "active member" of the Gesellschaft der Musikfreunde. His song *Erlafsee*, D.586 is the first to be published as a supplement to an almanac, the *Mahlerisches Taschenbuch*. Performance of his First Symphony by a Viennese orchestral society. Schubert's Overture D.591 is mentioned in the *Leipziger Allgemeine Musikzeitung*. Summer stay in Zseliz at the invitation of Prince Esterházy. Assassination of Kotzebue. Birth of Karl Marx. Beginning of the *Abendunterhaltungen* (musical soirees) of the Gesellschaft der Musikfreunde. Birth of Gounod. Beethoven begins writing the *Missa solemnis* and the *Hammerklavier* Sonata. Rossini's *Moisè in Egitto* first performed in Naples.

1819   First public performance of a Schubert song: *Schäfers Klage*, D. 121. With his *Prometheus*, D.451, Schubert's music appears for the first time on a program at the home of I. v. Sonnleithner. Vogl has *Die Zwillingsbrüder*, D.647, submitted to the Kärntnertortheater. First performance of *Das Dörfchen*, a quartet, at Sonnleithner's. Accompanied by Vogl Schubert travels to Upper Austria. Censorship becomes stricter. Schopenhauer completes his *The World as Will and Idea*. Founding of the Concerts Spirituels in Vienna. Beethoven begins to make use of "conversation books." Weber composes *Invitation to the Dance*. Rossini's *Otello* given at the Kärntnertortheater. Birth of Franz von Suppé.

1820 Schubert is accused of conspiratory activities with student groups and is arrested in the apartment of his friend Senn but soon released. Ferdinand Schubert becomes choir director in Altlerchenfeld; Schubert conducts Haydn's "Lord Nelson" Mass there. Performance of *Die Zwillingsbrüder* at the Kärntnertortheater and of *Die Zauberharfe,* D.644, at the theater an der Wien. First performance of *Erlkönig,* D.328, at Sonnleithner's. Composition of *Lazarus,* D.689, and the string quartet movement in C Minor, D.703. Journals in Leipzig and Dresden mention Schubert as a composer of songs. Death of Clemens Maria Hofbauer. Grillparzer completes his *Medea,* Walter Scott his *Ivanhoe.* Rossini's *Barber of Seville* given at the Kärntnertortheater.

1821 Schubert briefly employed as vocal coach at the Court Opera. First "Schubertiad" with Schubert songs. Vogl sings *Erlkönig* in a concert in the Kärntnertortheater. Schubert's friends arrange the publication of several of his songs by Cappi & Diabelli, on a commission basis. Johann Nestroy participates for the first time, as a bass singer, in a performance of Schubert's vocal quartet *Das Dörfchen,* D.598. Sketches for several symphonies; composition of dances. Metternich becomes chancellor. Birth of Charles Baudelaire, Gustave Flaubert, Feodor M. Dostoievsky. Domenico Barbaja leases the Kärntnertortheater; Spohr's *Zemire und Azor* performed there. First performance of Weber's *Preziosa* in Berlin.

1822 Schubert composes the opera *Alfonso und Estrella,* D.732, the Symphony in B Minor, D.759, and the

Mass in A Flat, D.678, an homage to the Emperor with the Hymn, D.748, for the musical "academy" (concert) at the Theresianum. He dedicates his Variations, Op.10, D.624 to Beethoven. First detailed article about Schubert as a composer of Lieder in the *Wiener Zeitschrift für Kunst, Literatur, Theater und Mode.* Beginning of the "reading circles" at Schober's. Beethoven is made an honorary member of the Music Society of Styria. Inauguration of the Josefstadt Theater with Beethoven's overture *The Consecration of the House.* Rossini stagione at the Kärntnertortheater. Weber gives a concert in Vienna; Liszt first performs there.

1823　Schubert is awarded honorary diplomas by the music societies of Graz and Linz. Illness and stay in the General Hospital. Composition of the opera *Fierabras,* D.796, and the incidental music for *Rosamunde,* D.797. First performance of *Rosamunde* at the Theater an der Wien. He composes the song cycle *Die schöne Müllerin,* D.795. First published collections of dances. Falling out with Cappi & Diabelli. Ricordi announces its *Biblioteca di musica moderna,* which includes Schubert. Death of Z. Werner. Friedrich Rückert writes his *Liebesfrühling.* First performance of Weber's *Euryanthe* at the Kärntnertortheater and of Rossini's *Semiramide* in Venice.

1824　Publication of the cycle *Die schöne Müllerin;* composition of String Quartet in A Minor, D.804, and Grand Duo, D.812. Second sojourn in Zseliz. Ferdinand Schubert appointed teacher at the Normal School. Death of M v. Collin. Birth of Bruckner and Smetana. Beethoven gives concert at the Kärntnertortheater; Ninth Symphony and parts of *Missa Solemnis* on program. End of Barbaja's lease of Kärntnertortheater. First performance of Meyerbeer's *Il Crociato in Egitto* in Venice. Lanner forms his own string orchestra playing in the *Erstes Kaffeehaus* in the Prater. The *Allgemeine musikalische Zeitung* ceases publication.

1825 W. A. Rieder completes Schubert portrait. Schubert's letter to Goethe remains unanswered. He begins composing the "Great" Symphony in C Major, D.944; travels to Steyr, Linz, Salzburg, and Gastein. Publication of the Mass in C Major, D.452. He is elected as an "alternate" to the board of the Gesellschaft der Musikfreunde. Death of Jean Paul. First performance of Grillparzer's *König Ottokars Glück und Ende* at the Theater an der Wien. Birth of Johann Strauss, Jr. Separation of Johann Strauss, Sr. and Josef Lanner. First performance by Schuppanzigh of Beethoven's String Quartet Op.127; private first performance of the Quartet Op.132. Beethoven becomes an honorary member of the Gesellschaft der Musikfreunde.

1826 Schubert applies unsuccessfully for the position of Vice-Hofkapellmeister. Hans Georg Nägeli mentions Schubert in his lectures; his plan to have Schubert included in the *Musikalische Ehrenpforte* does not materialize. Schubert contacts the German publishers H. Probst and Breitkopf & Härtel, with no results. The C Major Symphony is presented to the Gesellschaft der Musikfreunde; Schubert receives a stipend "in recognition of his achievements and for further encouragement." Death of Weber; first performance of his *Oberon* in London. Barbaja once more leases the Kärntnertortheater; I. Mosel becomes director of both court theaters. Public performance of Beethoven's Quartet Op.132.

1827   Schubert becomes board member of the Gesellschaft der Musikfreunde, participates in a concert in Graz. Composition of *Winterreise*, D.911 and of the Piano Trios in B-Flat Major, D.898 [according to recent investigations 1828] and E-Flat Major, D.929, and of the Impromptus, D.899. He begins work on the opera *Der Graf von Gleichen*, D.918. The C Major Symphony is copied for the Gesellschaft der Musikfreunde. I. Schuppanzigh performs Schubert's Octet, D.803. Heine completes his *Buch der Lieder*. Death of Beethoven. Birth of Josef Strauss. Johann Strauss, Sr. plays at the inn *Zu den zwei Täuberln*. Lanner composes his first waltzes entitled *Mitternachtswalzer*. Sigismund Thalberg gives a benefit concert in Vienna. A mutilated version of Weber's *Oberon* is given in the Theater in der Josefstadt. First performance of Bellini's *Il Pirata* in Milan.

1828   Last "Schubertiad" at J. Spaun's. Schubert gives his first and only concert consisting entirely of his own works. Ties to the publisher Probst in Leipzig are established. Composition of the Mass in E-Flat Major, D.950, *Schwanengesang*, D.957, and the three great piano sonatas D.958, 959, 960. Sketches for a large symphony, D.936 A. Illness and death. Memorial services and obituaries. Birth of Ibsen and Tolstoy. First performance of Goethe's *Faust* in Braunschweig. Niccolò Paganini reaps spectacular successes on concert tours that take him to Vienna. First public appearance of the nine-year-old Clara Wieck. Johann Nepomuk Hummel publishes his *Klavierschule*; Carl Czerny publishes his etudes for piano. First performance of Auber's *La muette de Portici* in Paris. Bellini's *Il Pirata* given at the Kärntnertortheater.

Notes

Instead of a Preface:

1. Franz Schubert. Neue Ausgabe sämtlicher Werke, hrsg. v. d. Internationalen Schubert-Gesellschaft, Kassel etc. 1964ff.

2. A few recent studies: O. Biba, Einige neue und wichtige Schubertiana im Archiv der Gesellschaft der Musikfreunde, in: Österreichische Musikzeitschrift 33 (1978), 604–610; E. Hilmar, Neue Funde, Daten und Dokumente zum symphonischen Werk Franz Schuberts, in: Österreichische Musikzeitschrift 33 (1978), 266–276; R. Winter, Paper studies and the future of Schubert research, in: Problems of style and chronology (Schubert Studies), ed. by E. Badura-Skoda and P. Branscombe, Cambridge 1982, 209–275.

3. R. H. *Bartsch,* Schwammerl, Leipzig, n. d.

4. Schubert. Die Dokumente seines Lebens. Gesammelt und erläutert v. O. E. *Deutsch,* Leipzig 1964. Cited as: Dokumente. *Translator's note:* The Dokumente are easily available in an English translation: *The Schubert Reader,* O. E. Deutsch, editor, Eric Blom, Transl. New York, Norton, 1947.

5. Schubert. Erinnerungen seiner Freunde. Gesammelt u. hrsg. v. O. E. *Deutsch,* Leipzig 1966. Cited as: Erinnerungen.

6. Franz Schubert. Thematisches Verzeichnis seiner Werke in chronologischer Folge, v. O. E. *Deutsch.* Neuausgabe in deutscher Sprache bearb, u. hrsg. v. d. Editionsleitung der Neuen Schubert-Ausgabe und W. Aderhold, Kassel etc. 1978.

7. The exhibition catalogue „Haydn und seine Zeit", ed. by G. Mraz u. G. Schlag, Eisenstadt 1982, is an example.

127

Schubert's Years of Apprenticeship

1. J. *Rossi,* Denkbuch für Fürst und Vaterland, 1814. See also Franz Schubert und seine Zeit, exhibition catalogue, ed. by O. Biba, Wien 1978, 60.

2. E. *Hilmar,* Ferdinand Schuberts Skizze zu einer Autobiographie, in: Schubert-Studien (Österreichische Akademie der Wissenschaften, Sitzungsberichte, 341. Bd., H. 19), ed. by F. Grasberger and O. Wessely, Wien 1978, 85–117.

3. In private Swiss archives. Information supplied by Walter Dürr of the Internationale Schubert-Gesellschaft and Hans Schneider, Tutzing.

4. F. *Rochlitz,* Für Freunde der Tonkunst, vol. 4, ed. by A. Dörffel, Leipzig 1868.

5. O. E. *Deutsch,* Das k. u. k. Stadtkonvikt in Schuberts Zeit. Nach Akten des Wiener Staatsarchives, in: Die Quelle 78 (1928), 4, 479.

6. E. *Hanslick,* Geschichte des Concertwesens in Wien, 1. Teil, Wien 1869, 172f.

7. Dokumente, 88f.

8. E. *Hilmar,* Datierungsprobleme im Werk Schuberts, in: Schubertkongress-Bericht, ed. by O. Brusatti, Graz 1979, 48.

9. Franz Schubert und seine Zeit, exhibition catalogue ed. by O. Biba, Wien 1978, 61.

From Musical Salon to *Schubertiade*

1. I. *Mosel,* Übersicht des gegenwärtigen Zustandes der Tonkunst in Wien, in: Vaterländische Blätter für den Österreichischen Kaiserstaat 1, Wien 1808, 39.

2. V. *Tornius,* Salons. Bilder gesellschaftlicher Kultur aus fünf Jahrhunderten, vol. 2, Leipzig 1918, 226.

3. C. *Pichler,* Denkwürdigkeiten aus meinem Leben, ed. by E. K. Blümml, vol. 1, München, 1914, 294.

4. O. *Biba,* Franz Schubert in den musikalischen Abendunterhaltungen der Gesellschaft der Musikfreunde, in: Schubert-Studien (Österreichische Akademie der Wissenschaften, Sitzungsberichte, 341. Bd., H. 19), ed. by F. Grasberger and O. Wessely, Wien 1978, 7–31.

5. The collection today belongs to the Gesellschaft der Musikfreunde, Vienna.

6. R. *Krüger*, Biedermeier. Eine Lebenshaltung zwischen 1815 und 1848, Wien 1979, 169.

7. L. v. *Sonnleithner*, Musikalische Skizzen aus Alt-Wien (Recensionen und Mittheilungen über Theater und Musik 7), Wien 1861.

8. See also Fritz v. Hartmann's notes of March 4, 1827: Dokumente, 413.

9. Dokumente, 485f.

10. See also 94f.

Schubert and the Publishers

1. H. *Gericke*, Der Wiener Musikalienhandel von 1700–1778, Graz 1960; Carl *Junker*, Korporation der Wiener Buch-, Kunst- und Musikalienhändler, Wien 1907; see also A. *Weinmann*, Wiener Musikverleger und Musikalienhändler von Mozarts Zeit bis gegen 1860 (Österreichische Akademie der Wissenschaften, Sitzungsberichte, 230. Bd.), Wien 1956.

2. E. *Hilmar*, Der Musikalienhandel in der Zeit der Wiener Hochklassik (Wiener Kulturnotizen), Wien 1972.

3. Cited from the announcement, see note 2.

4. O. E. *Deutsch*, Schuberts Verleger, in: Der Bär, Leipzig 1928, 14.

5. Schubert's first printed work, the song *Erlafsee*, D.586, appeared as a supplement to the *Mahlerisches Taschenbuch*, Vienna, 1818. The song *Widerschein*, D.639, was published 1820/21 in W. G. Becker's *Taschenbuch zum geselligen Vergnügen*, Leipzig.

6. Original in the Handschriftensammlung of the Wiener Stadt- und Landesbibliothek. Partially published in: Franz Schubert, Katalog zur Ausstellung, ed. by E. Hilmar und O. Brusatti, Wien 1978, Nr. 151.

7. Franz Schubert und seine Zeit, exhibition catalogue, ed. by O. Biba, Wien 1978, 52.

8. Dokumente, 129.

9. Letter of 21 September 1824; Dokumente, 259.

10. Letter of 12 November 1822; Dokumente 169.

11. Schubert to Leopold Kupelwieser, 31 March 1824; Dokumente 235.

12. A. *Weinmann,* Verlagsverzeichnis Senefelder, Steiner, Haslinger, Vol. 1 (Vorwort), München - Salzburg 1979, 5.

13. R. *Hilmar,* Der Musikverlag Artaria & Comp. Geschichte und Probleme der Druckproduktion, Tutzing 1977, 65ff.

14. *Ibid.* 64.

15. B. Schott's Söhne to Schubert, 9 February 1828; Dokumente, 493.

Concert Life in Vienna

1. E. *Hanslick,* Geschichte des Concertwesens in Wien, 1. Teil, Wien 1869, 145.

2. *Ibid.* 144.

3. *Ibid.* 148.

4. C. *Pichler,* Denkwürdigkeiten aus meinem Leben, ed. by E.-K. Blümml, vol. 2, München 1914, 42.

5. O. *Biba,* Franz Schubert in den musikalischen Abendunterhaltungen der Gesellschaft der Musikfreunde, in: Schubert-Studien (Österreichische Akademie der Wissenschaften, Sitzungsberichte, 341. Bd., H. 19), ed. by F. Grasberger and O. Wessely, Wien 1978, 7–31.

6. *Ibid.* 7.

7. Cited after Hanslick, *op. cit.,* 187.

8. *Ibid.* 215.

9. F. A. *Kanne,* Über die Privat Concerte in Wien, in: Conversationsblatt 2 (1820), Nr. 57, 551–555.

10. *Ibid.*

11. Allgemeine Theaterzeitung, Wien, 29 March 1821.

12. See Note 9.

13. Allgemeine Theaterzeitung, Wien 1 June 1824, 264.

14. Allgemeine Theaterzeitung, Wien 26 April 1827, 203.

15. See Note 9.

Contrasts

1. Concerning the history of the Theater an der Wien see A. *Bauer*, 150 Jahre Theater an der Wien, Zürich - Leipzig - Wien 1952.

2. Cited after F. *Reischl*, Wien zur Biedermeierzeit. Volksleben in Wiens Vorstädten nach zeitgenössischen Schilderungen, Wien 1921, 172f.

3. *Ibid.*, 177f.

4. Concerning the dating of the opera *Adrast* see E. *Hilmar*, Verzeichnis der Schubert-Handschriften in der Musiksammlung der Wiener Stadt- und Landesbibliothek (Catalogus musicus VIII), Kassel etc. 1978, 17.

5. C. Dahlhaus in *Rossini und die Restauration*. (Die Musik des 19. Jahrhunderts, Neues Handbuch der Musikwissenschaft, vol. 6, 47ff.).

6. Schubert's letter to F. v. Schober, 30 November 1823; Dokumente 207.

7. Letter of 4 August 1828 to Seidl; Dokumente, 530.

8. Dokumente, 165; concerning the history of the Leopoldstädter Theater siehe F. *Hadamowsky*, Das Theater in der Wiener Leopoldstadt 1781–1860 (Katalog der Theatersammlung der Nationalbibliothek in Wien, vol. III).

9. *Hadamowsky*, 63.

10. A. *Bauer*, Das Theater in der Josefstadt zu Wien, Wien - München 1957.

11. *Ibid.*, 55.

12. F. *Hadamowsky*, Die Wiener Hoftheater (Staatstheater), Teil 2: Die Wiener Hofoper (Staatsoper) 1811–1974 (Museion 1. Reihe, Bd. 4), Wien 1975, p. VII.

13. See p. 63.

14. Dokumente 91.

15. The libretto is in the Handschriftensammlung der Wiener Stadt- und Landesbibliothek.

16. Dokumente, 201, 204.

17. Letter of 31 March 1824; Dokumente, 234.

18. Letter of 30 November 1823; Dokumente, 207.

19. Dokumente, 197.

20. Letter of 20. October 1824 to Count Esterházy; Dokumente, 262. Engl. ed. p. 381.

21. Dokumente, 260f.

22. Details in E. *Hilmar,* Verzeichnis der Schubert-Handschriften, 28f.

Schubert and Dance Music

1. J. F. *Reichardt,* Vertraute Briefe. Introduction and notes by G. Gugitz, vol. 3, München 1918, 332.

2. Graf de la Garde, Gemälde des Wiener Congresses 1814–1815. Erinnerungen, Feste, Sittenschilderungen, Anecdoten. Transl. by L. Eichler, Leipzig 1844, vol. 3, 125f.

3. Fasching in Wien. Der Wiener Walzer 1750–1850. Exhibition catalogue, ed. by R. Witzmann, Wien 1979, 5.

4. Dekret der k. k. Polizeidirektion, 20 August 1820. (Ch. *Fauller,* Gesetze, Verordnungen und Vorschriften, vol. 4).

5. R. *Klein,* Schubertstätten, Wien 1972, 79f.

6. Fasching in Wien, 8.

7. J. *Gerning,* Reise durch Österreich und Italien, Part I, Frankfurt (n.d.), 30.

8. *Graf de la Garde, op. cit.,* vol. 1, 64f.

9. R. *Flotzinger,* Und walzen umatum... Zur Genealogie des Wiener Walzers, in: Österreichische Musikzeitschrift 30 (1975), 505–515 and 573–578.

10. F. *Lange,* Franz Schubert und die Tanzmusik seiner Zeit, Wien 1906.

11. The *XII Tänze componirt für den Apollo Saal im Jahr 1809* serve as an example, published by *Kunst und Industrie Comptoir,* Wien.

12. M. *Schönherr* and K. *Reinöhl,* Johann Strauss Vater. Ein Werkverzeichnis, London - Wien -Zürich 1954, 12.

The Literary Scene

1. E. *Bauernfeld,* Aus Alt- und Neu-Wien (Gesammelte Schriften, vol. 9), Wien 1873, 202. Bauernfeld described the *„gepriesene österreichische System"* as *„rein negatives: die Furcht vor dem Geiste, die Negation des Geistes, der absolute Stillstand, die Versumpfung, die Verdummung"*. (*Ibid.,* 205)

2. H. *Seidler,* Österreichischer Vormärz und

Goethezeit. Geschichte einer literarischen Auseinandersetzung (Österreichische Akademie der Wissenschaften, Sitzungsberichte, 394. Nr. 6), Wien 1982, 55.

3. H. L. *Mikoletzky,* Österreich. Das entscheidende 19. Jahrhundert. Geschichte, Kultur, Wirtschaft, Wien 1972, 233.

4. *Seidler, loc. cit.* 167.

5. Dokumente, 34.

6. *Seidler, op. cit.,* 245.

7. R. *Van Hoorickx,* Textänderungen in Schuberts Messen, in: Schubert-Kongress-Bericht, ed. by O. Brusatti, Graz 1979, 249f.

8. W. *Scherer,* Geschichte der deutschen Literatur, Wien 1948, 484f.

9. Cited after *Mikoletzky, op. cit.* 249.

10. Undated document in the Handschriftensammlung der Wiener Stadt- und Landesbibliothek.

11. *Seidler, op. cit.,* 195f.

12. *Mikoletzky, op. cit.,* 235.

13. Letter of 30 November 1823; Dokumente 207.

14. Dokumente, 479, 494, 499.

15. Diary and letters of Wilhelm Müller, ed. by Ph. S. Allen and J. T. Hatfield, Chicago 1903, 125.

16. Letter of 14 August 1823; Dokumente, 197.

17. Letter of 21 July 1825; Dokumente, 296.

18. Letter by Ottenwalt to J. v. Spaun, 27 July 1825; Dokumente, 303. Engl. ed. p. 442.

Schubert the Composer

1. Letter of 12 October 1818; Dokumente, 71.

2. E. *Krenek,* Franz Schubert und wir, in: Bericht über den internationalen Kongress für Schubert-Forschung, Wien 1928, 72.

3. Letter by Holzapfel to Stadler, 22 February 1822; Dokumente, 148.

4. Letter by Schwind to Schober, 7 January 1825; Dokumente, 271.

5. Letter by Traweger to Schubert, 19 May 1828; Dokumente, 517.

6. Letter of 27 September 1827; Dokumente, 451f.

7. O. *Biba,* Franz Schubert und die Gesellschaft der Musikfreunde in Wien, in: Schubert-Kongress-Bericht, edited by O. Brusatti, Graz 1979, 23f.

8. *Ibid.,* 24.

9. *Ibid.,* 25.

10. See note 8.

11. Allgemeine musikalische Zeitung, Wien, 16 April 1823, 246.

12. Dokumente, 112.

13. The review appeared on 19 January, 1821; Dokumente, 145.

14. Dokumente, 150ff.

15. Dokumente, 345.

16. Letter by Nägeli to Karl Czerny, 18 June, 1826; Dokumente, 364.

17. Dokumente, 348ff.

18. Dokumente, 533.

19. Rochlitz to I. Mosel, 30 April 1826; Dokumente, 356.

20. Dokumente, 468.

21. *Ibid.*

22. Dokumente, 521.

23. Letter of 2 December 1824; Dokumente, 265f.

24. Schubert to Kupelwieser, letter of 31 March 1824; Dokumente, 235.

25. Concerning the dating of the C Major Symphony, D.944, see the following studies: O. *Biba,* Franz Schubert und die Gesellschaft der Musikfreunde, *op. cit.,* 28ff.; E. *Hilmar,* Datierungsprobleme im Werk Schuberts, in: Schubert-Kongress-Bericht, ed. by O. Brusatti, Graz 1979, 57ff.; R. *Winter,* Paper studies on the future of Schubert research, in: Problems of style and chronology (Schubert Studies), ed. by E. Badura-Skoda and P. Branscombe, Cambridge 1982, 209ff.—The authors agree that work on the symphony began already in 1825, not in 1828. The editors of the new Complete Schubert Edition now have accepted that belief. Opinions still differ on the complex question whether Schubert began to write down the symphony in the spring, or not until summer. To rely on stylistic considerations alone for dating the work "only late in 1825," as Harry Goldschmidt did (Beiträge zur Musik-

wissenschaft, Heft 4, 1979) is more than questionable. For Goldschmidt, however, this was the only way to defend his theory about the existence of a separate "Gmunden" Symphony.

26. See also Franz Schubert. Drei Symphonie-Fragmente. Faksimile-Erstdruck, published by the Wiener Stadt-und Landesbibliothek, Postscript by E. Hilmar (Documenta Musicologica VI), Kassel etc. 1978.

27. Franz Schubert und seine Zeit. Exhibition catalogue ed by O. Biba, Wien 1978, 63.

28. Dokumente, 327. Engl. p. 477.

29. A. Milder to Schubert, letter of 8 March, 1825; Dokumente, 280.

30. See p. 98.

Bibliography

I. General

1. History, Literature, Music, Theater

Ph. S. *Allen* - J. T. *Hatfield* (ed.), Diary and Letters of Wilhelm Müller, with explanatory notes and a biographical Index, Chicago 1903.

A. *Bauer*, 150 Jahre Theater an der Wien, Zürich - Leipzig -Wien 1952.

————, Opern und Operetten in Wien. Verzeichnis ihrer Erstaufführung in der Zeit von 1629 bis zur Gegenwart, Graz - Köln 1955.

————, Das Theater in der Josefstadt zu Wien, Wien - München 1957.

R. *Bauer*, Der Idealismus und seine Gegner in Österreich (Beiheft 3 zum Euphorion), Heidelberg 1966.

————, Grillparzers „Ahnfrau". Ihre Kritiker und ihr Publikum, Grillparzer Forum Forchtenstein 1973.

C. *Baumann*, Wilhelm Müller, The poet of the Schubert song cycles. His life and works, London 1981.

E. *Behler*, Friedrich Schlegel - Schriften und Fragmente. Ein Gesamtbild seines Geistes, Stuttgart 1956.

C. *Dahlhaus*, Die Musik des 19. Jahrhunderts (Neues Handbuch der Musikwissenschaft, vol. 6), Wiesbaden - Laaber 1980.

————, (ed.) Studien zur Trivialmusik des 19. Jahrhunderts, Regensburg 1967.

F. *Hadamowsky*, Das theater in der Wiener Leopoldstadt 1781– 1860 (Kataloge der Theatersammlung der Nationalbibliothek in Wien, vol. 3), Wien 1934.

_____ , Das Wiener Hoftheater (Staatstheater) (Museion I, vol. 4), Part 2: Die Wiener Hofoper (Staatsoper) 1811–1974, Wien 1975.

E. *Hanslick,* Geschichte des Concertwesens in Wien (Part 1), Wien 1869.

E. *Horner,* Eduard Bauernfeld, Leipzig - Berlin - Wien 1900.

K. *Kobald,* Alt-Wiener Musikstätten, Zürich - Leipzig - Wien 1919.

J. *Körner,* Briefe von und an August Wilhelm Schlegel, 2 vols., Zürich 1930.

H. *Kunze,* Lieblings-Bücher von dazumal. Eine Blütenlese aus den erfolgreichsten Büchern von 1750–1860, München, 1938.

H. L. *Mikoletzky,* Österreich. Das entscheidende 19. Jahrhundert. Geschichte, Kultur und Wirtschaft, Wien 1972.

I. F. *Mosel,* Über das Leben und die Werke des Anton Salieri, Wien 1827.

O. *Rommel,* Die Alt-Wiener Volkskomödie, Wien 1952.

R. *Rosenberg,* Literaturverhältnisse im deutschen Vormärz, Berlin 1975.

G. *Schilling,* Das musikalische Europa oder Sammlung von durchgehends authentischen Lebensnachrichten über jetzt in Europa lebende ausgezeichnete Tonkünstler, Musikgelehrte, Componisten, Virtuosen, Sänger etc., Speyer 1842.

J. *Schreyvogel,* Biographie Schillers und Anleitung zur Critic seines Werks, Wien 1810.

_____ , Tagebücher 1810–1823 (Schriften der Gesellschaft für Theatergeschichte vols. 2 and 3), Berlin 1903.

H. *Seidler,* Österreichischer Vormärz und Goethezeit. Geschichte einer literarischen Auseinandersetzung (Österreichische Akademie der Wissenschaften, Sitzungsberichte, vol. 394), Wien 1982.

F. *Sengle,* Biedermeierzeit. Deutsche Literatur im Spannungsfeld zwischen Restauration und Revolution 1815 und 1848, Stuttgart 1971.

H. *Srbik,* Metternich. Der Staatsmann und der Mensch, 2 vols. München 1925.

A. *Weinmann,* Wiener Musikverleger und Musikalienhändler von Mozarts Zeit bis gegen 1860 (Österreichische Akademie der Wissenschaften, Sitzungsberichte, vol.

230), Wien 1956.

———— , Der Alt-Wiener Musikverlag im Spiegel der „Wiener Zeitung" (Publikationen des Instituts für Österreichische Musikdokumentation 2), Tutzing 1976.

E. *Winter*, Romantismus, Restauration und Frühliberalismus im österreichischen Vormärz, Wien 1968.

2. Cultural History, Painting, Dance

E. V. *Bauernfeld*, Aus Alt- und Neu-Wien (Gesammelte Schriften 9), Wien 1873.

W. *Bietak*, Das Lebensgefühl des Biedermeier in der österreichischen Dichtung, Wien 1931.

G. *Böhmer*, Die Welt des Biedermeier, München 1968.

I. F. *Castelli*, Memoiren meines Lebens - Gefundenes und Empfundenes, Erlebtes und Erstrebtes, 4 vols., Wien - Prag 1861.

R. *Feuchtmüller* - W. *Mrazek*, Biedermeier in Österreich, Wien - Hannover - Bern 1963.

R. *Flotzinger*, Landlerisch tanzen, in: Österreichische Musikzeitschrift 29 (1974), 463–474.

———— , Und walzen umatum ... Zur Genealogie des Wiener Walzers, in: Österreichische Musikzeitschrift 30 (1975), 505–515, 572–578.

H. *Funck*, Musikalisches Biedermeier, in: Deutsche Vierteljahrsschrift für Literaturwissenschaft und Geistesgeschichte, vol. 14 (1936).

W. *Geismeier*, Malerei des Biedermeier, Leipzig 1973.

F. *Glück* (ed.), Moritz v. Schwind und seine Vaterstadt (Exhibition catalogue), Wien 1954.

Graf de la Garde, Gemälde des Wiener Congresses 1814–1815. Erinnerungen, Feste, Sittenschilderungen, Anecdoten, 4 vols. Transl. by L. Eichler, Leipzig 1844.

F. *Gräffer*, Kleine Wiener Memoiren und Wiener Dosenstücke, ed. by A. Schlosser, and G. Gugitz, 2 vols., München 1918 and 1922.

M. *Greiner*, Zwischen Biedermeier und Bourgeoisie, Göttingen 1953.

G. *Hermann*, Das Biedermeier im Spiegel seiner Zeit. Briefe, Tagebücher, Memoiren, Volksszenen und ähnliche

138

Dokumente, [no place], 1913.

V. *Junk,* Handbuch des Tanzes, Stuttgart 1930.

E. *Kalkschmidt,* Biedermeiers Glück und Ende, München 1957.

F. *Klingenbeck,* Das Walzerbuch. Historisches und Bezauberndes vom Wiener Walzer, Wien 1952.

L. *Knessl,* Musik im Biedermeier. Kulturhistorisches Feuilleton, Linz n. d.

R. *Krüger,* Biedermeier. Eine Lebenshaltung zwischen 1815 und 1848, 2d ed., Wien 1982.

R. *Lach,* Zur Geschichte des Gesellschaftstanzes im 18. Jahrhundert (Museion, vol. 1), Wien 1920.

F. *Lange,* Josef Lanner und Johann Strauss. Ihre Zeit, ihr Leben und ihre Werke, 2d ed. Leipzig 1919.

W. *Lhotsky* (Ed.), Künstler aus dem Schubert-Kreis. Catalogue of the 36th exhibition of the Bibliothek der Akademie der Bildenden Künste in Wien, Wien 1978.

A. T. *Leitich,* Wiener Biedermeier. Kultur, Kunst und Leben der alten Kaiserstaadt vom Wiener Kongress bis zum Sturmjahr 1848, Bielefeld - Leipzig 1941.

A. *Liess,* Johann Michael Vogl. Hofoperist und Schubert-Sänger, Graz - Köln 1954.

J. *Mailáth* (ed.), Leben der Sophie Müller, und nachgelassene Papiere, Wien 1832.

I. L. *Mendelssohn,* Zur Entwicklung des Walzers, in: Studien zur Musikwissenschaft 13 (1926).

F. *Patzer* (ed.), Wiener Kongresstagebuch 1814/1815 [by M. F. Perth] (Veröffentlichungen aus der Wiener Stadt- und Landesbibliothek 8, Wiener Schriften 50), Wien 1981.

C. *Pichler,* Denkwürdigkeiten aus meinem Leben, ed. by E. K. Blümml, 2 vols., München 1914.

F. *Racek* (ed.). Johann Strauss (Exhibition catalogue), Wien 1975.

J. F. *Reichardt,* Vertraute Briefe auf einer Reise nach Wien und den österreichischen Staaten zu Ende des Jahres 1808 und zu Anfang 1809. Introduction by G. Gugitz, 2 vols., München 1918.

P. F. *Schmidt,* Biedermeier-Malerei. Zur Geschichte und Geistigkeit der deutschen Malerei in der ersten Hälfte des 19. Jahrhunderts, München, 1923.

M. *Schönherr-J. Ziegler,* Aus der Zeit des Wiener Walzers. Titelblätter zu Tanzkompositionen der Walzerfamilie Strauss, erläutert, datiert und mit Randbemerkungen versehen. Dortmund 1981.

M. *Schönherr,* Lanner-Strauss-Ziehrer. Synoptisches Handbuch der Tänze und Märsche, Wien - München 1982.

S. *Schutte,* Der Ländler. Untersuchungen zur musikalischen Struktur ungeradtaktiger österreichischer Volkstänze (Sammlung musikwissenschaftlicher Abhandlungen 52), Strasbourg 1970.

H. *Tietze,* Alt-Wien in Wort und Bild, Wien 1926.

V. *Tornius,* Salons. Bilder gesellschaftlicher Kultur aus fünf Jahrhunderten, 2 vols., Leipzig 1918 (3d ed.).

R. *Witzmann* (ed.), Fasching in Wien. Der Wiener Walzer 1750–1850 (Catalogue of exhibition), Wien 1979.

II. Literature about Schubert

1. Work lists, Catalogues, Documents, Anthologies

Thematisches Verzeichnis der im Druck erschienenen werke v. Franz Schubert, ed. by G. Nottebohm, Wien 1874.

Schubert, Thematic Catalogue of all his works in chronological order, by O. E. Deutsch, London 1951.

Franz Schubert. Thematisches Verzeichnis seiner Werke in chronologischer Folge, v. O. E. Deutsch. New ed. in German, edited and published by the Editionsleitung der Neuen Schubert-Ausgabe u. W. Aderhold, Kassel etc. 1978.

E. *Hilmar,* Verzeichnis der Schubert-Handschriften in der Musiksammlung der Wiener Stadt- und Landes-bibliothek (Catalogus Musicus 8), Kassel etc. 1978.

Schubert-Ausstellung der Stadt Wien, verbunden mit einer Ausstellung von Werken der maler Moritz v. Schwind, Josef Danhauser und Leopold Kupelwieser, Wien 1897.

Schubert-Zentenarausstellung der Stadt Wien (Catalogue), Wien 1928.

Franz Schubert und seine Zeit. Ausstellung im Archiv der Gesellschaft der Musikfreunde in Wien, Catalogue by O. Biba, Wien 1978.

Franz Schubert. Ausstellung der Wiener Stadt- und Landes-bibliothek zum 150. Todestag des Komponisten,

Catalogue ed. by E. Hilmar u. O. Brusatti, with an introduction by W. Obermaier, Wien 1978.

Franz Schubert in Kunst und Kitsch, Catalogue by H. N. Wolf, Wien 1978.

Franz Schubert. Die Dokumente seines Lebens, ed. by O. E. Deutsch, München 1914.

Schubert. A documentary biography by O. E. Deutsch. Translated by Eric Blom, London 1946, N.Y. 1947.

Schubert. Die Dokumente seines Lebens, gesammelt u. erläutert v. O. E. Deutsch, Kassel 1964.

Franz Schubert. Sein Leben in Bildern, ed. by O. E. Deutsch, München 1913.

Franz Schuberts Briefe und Schriften, ed. by O. E. Deutsch, München 1919.

Schubert. Zeugnisse seiner Zeitgenossen, ed. by O. E. Deutsch, Frankfurt/M. 1964.

Schubert. Die Erinnerungen seiner Freunde, gesammelt u. hrsg. v. O. E. Deutsch, Leipzig 1966.

W. *Obermaier*, Franz Schubert, Brief an die Freunde. English version by P. Catty, Wien 1979.

W. *Reich*, Schubert-Brevier. Aus den Dokumenten seines Lebens (Vom Dauernden in der Zeit 49), Zürich 1949.

H. *Rutz*, Franz Schubert. Dokumente seines Lebens und Schaffens, München 1952.

Schubert issue of the Zeitschrift „Die Musik" 6., Berlin 1906/07 (with contributions by v. Perger, O. E. Deutsch, F. A. Geisler, E. Mandyczewski, L. Schmidt and others).

Bericht über den Internationalen Kongress für Schubertforschung 1928 (ed. by R. Haas and A. Orel), Augsburg 1929 (with contributions by O. E. Deutsch, M. Friedländer, R. Haas, G. Kinsky, E. Krenek, R. Lach, P. Mies, P. Stefan and others).

Schubert-Kongress Wien 1978. Report ed. by O. Brusatti, Graz 1979 (with contributions by O. Biba, E. Budde, C. Dahlhaus, W. Dürr, H. Federhofer, A. Feil, H. Goldschmidt, G. Gruber, E. Hilmar, R. van Hoorickx, W. Obermaier and others).

Schubert-Studien. Festgabe der Österreichischen Akademie der Wissenschaften (Sitzungsberichte, vol. 341) ed. by F. Grasberger and O. Wessely, Wien 1978 (with contributions by O. Biba, O. Brusatti, W. Dürr, H. Federhofer, A. Feil, E. Hilmar, C. Höslinger, L. Kantner, W. Salmen, O. Wessely, I. Weinmann).

Franz Schubert. Sonderband der Musik-Konzepte, ed. by H.-K. Metzger and R. Riehn, München 1979 (with contributions by W. Dürr, R. Frisius, P. Gülke, R. Leibowitz, D. Schnebel and others).

Franz Schubert et la symphonie. Eléments d'une nouvelle perspective (La Revue musicale), ed. by P.-G. Langevin, Paris 1980/81 (with contributions by H. Halbreich, E. Hilmar, P.-G. Langevin, B. Newbould).

Problems of Style and Chronology (Schubert Studies), ed. by E. Badura-Skoda and P. Branscombe), Cambridge 1982 (with contributions by E. and P. Badura-Skoda, P. Branscombe, E. Brody, W. Dürr, A. Feil, M. Flothius, P. Gülke, R. Hallmark, R. van Hoorickx, N. Mckay, A. Weinmann, R. Winter, C. Wolff).

2. Monographs

K. *Adametz*, Franz Schubert in der Geschichte des Wiener Männergesang-Vereines, Wien [1938].

A. *Audley*, Franz Schubert. Sa vie et ses oeuvres, Paris 1871 (2d ed.).

F. *Bac*, Schubert ou le Harpe eolienne, Paris 1929.

A. B. *Bach*, The Art Ballad; Loewe and Schubert, Edinburgh - London 1890.

H. *Barbedette*, Franz Schubert. Sa vie, ses oeuvres, son temps, Paris 1865.

R. *Bates*, Franz Schubert, Edinburgh 1934.

M. *Bauer*, Die Lieder Franz Schuberts, Leipzig 1915.

A. C. *Bell*, The Songs of Schubert, London 1954.

A. *Benedikt*, Schubert-Legenden. With a preface by J. Redlin, Leipzig 1928.

R. *Benz*, Franz Schubert, der Vollender der deutschen Musik, Jena 1928.

H. *Berner*, Schwarzrotgoldene Schubertiade. Eine Rückschau, München 1959.

O. *Bie*, Franz Schubert. Sein Leben und sein Werk, Berlin 1925.

——— , A biography of Franz Schubert, New York 1928.

H. *Biehle,* Schuberts Lieder in Kritik und Literatur, Berlin 1928.
————— , Schuberts Lieder als Gesangsproblem (Musikalisches
    Magazin 74), Langensalza 1929.
H. M. *Böttcher,* Der Unvollendete. Franz Schubert und sein
    Kreis, Rudolfstadt 1954.
H. *Bosch,* Die Entwicklung des Romantischen in Schuberts
    Liedern, Borna-Leipzig 1930.
L. A. *Bourgault-Ducoudray,* Schubert. Biographie critique, Paris
    1926.
K. *Brachtel,* Schuberts musikalische Eigenart, Friedek 1915.
F. *Braun,* Schubert im Freundeskreis, Leipzig n.d.
A. *Brent-Smith,* Schubert, Quartett in D minor and Octet (The
    musical Pilgrim), Oxford 1927.
————— , Schubert, The symphonies (The musical Pilgrim),
    Oxford 1926.
M. J. E. *Brown,* Schubert's Variations, London - New York 1954.
————— , Schubert. A critical biography, London 1958.
————— , Schubert. Eine kritische Biographie, transl. by v. G.
    Sievers, Wiesbaden 1969.
————— , Essays on Schubert, New York 1966.
P. *Bülow,* Franz Schubert. Ein deutsches Musikerleben (Kranz-
    Bücherei 161), Frankfurt 1928.
E. *Buenzod,* Franz Schubert, Paris 1946 (2d ed.).
C. *Cassella,* Alcuni esempi dalle Versioni per i Lieder di
    Schubert, Roma 1966.
C. *Castello,* Vorüber . . . St. Pöltener Schubertiade, St. Pölten -
    Wien 1920.
A. *Chalus,* Schubert und seine h-moll-Sinfonie im Blickpunkt
    seiner Freundschaft mit Anselm Hüttenbrenner. Die
    neuen Forschungsergebnisse, Wien 1965.
M. T. *Chiesa,* Schubert. La vita. L'opera, Milano 1932.
J. *Chochlov,* O poslednem periode tvorcestva schuberta, Moskva
    1968.
G. R. *Cunningham,* Franz Schubert als Theaterkomponist (Diss.),
    Freiburg i. Breisgau 1974.
W. *Dahms,* Schubert, Berlin - Leipzig 1912.
F. V. *Damian,* Franz Schuberts Liederkreis „Die schöne
    Müllerin", Leipzig 1928.
O. E. *Deutsch,* Die Originalausgaben von Schuberts Goethe-
    Liedern. Ein musikbibliographischer Versuch, Wien
    1926.

_____ , Schubert und Grillparzer, Wien 1949.

C. *Dumont*, Franz Schubert. Wanderer zwischen den Zeiten, Braunschweig - Zürich 1978.

E. *Duncan*, Schubert. London 1905.

A. *Einstein*, Schubert. Ein musikalisches Porträt, Zürich 1952. (Also in English.)

H. *Eschmann*, Schubert-Beethoven, Ein stilkritischer Vergleich, Köln 1934.

H. *Eulenberg*, Schubert und die Frauen, Hellerau 1928.

F. *Farga*, Schubert. Ein Lebensbild, Wien 1947.

A. *Farinelli*, Beethoven e Schubert, Palermo 1929.

R. *Feigl*, Klar um Schubert. Beseitigung von Irrmeinungen, Fehlangaben usw., 2d ed. Linz 1938.

A. *Feil*, Studien zu Schuberts Rhythmik, München 1966.

_____ , Franz Schubert. „Die schöne Müllerin", „Winterreise". With an essay „Wilhelm Müller und die Romantik" by R. Vollmann, Stuttgart 1975.

N. *Flower*, Franz Schubert, London etc. 1928 (2d ed. 1949).

_____ , Franz Schubert. The Man and his circle, London etc. 1928.

E. *Frerichs*, Franz Schubert. Sein Leben. Sein Schaffen, Berlin (1924).

M. *Friedländer*, Franz Schubert. Skizze seines Lebens und Wirkens, Leipzig n. d.

H. F. *Frost*, Franz Schubert, London n. d. (2d ed.).

H. *Gál*, Schubert oder die Melodie, Frankfurt/M. 1970.

M. *Gallet*, Franz Schubert et le Lied, Paris 1907.

T. G. *Georgiades*, Schubert, Musik und Lyrik, Göttingen 1967.

Th. *Gérold*, Schubert, Paris 1923.

H. *Goldschmidt*, Franz Schubert, ein Lebensbild, Berlin 1954.

M. *Graefe* (ed.), Schubert und seine Dichter. 85 Liedtexte. With a Postscript by P. Petzoldt, Leipzig 1953.

E. M. *Grew*, Franz Schubert. A Sequence of Sonnets and a Poem Anthology, Birmingham 1928.

G. *Grove*, Beethoven, Schubert, Mendelssohn. With an Introduction by E. Blom, London 1951.

K. *Gutkas* (ed.), Schubert in Niederösterreich, St. Pölten 1978.

G. *Heinze*, Franz Schubert, Philadelphia 1908.

R. *Heuberger*, Franz Schubert (Berühmte Musiker 14), Berlin 1920 (3d ed.).

K. *Höcker*, Wege zu Schubert (Deutsche Musikbücherei 4),

Regensburg 1940.

F. *Hug,* Franz Schubert. Leben und Werk eines Frühvollendeten, Frankfurt/M. 1958.

K. *Huschke,* Das Siebengestirn der grossen Schubertschen Kammermusikwerke, Pritzwalk 1928.

A. *Hutchings,* Schubert (The Master Musicians), London 1945/47.

W. *Jaspert,* Franz Schubert. Zeugnisse seines irdischen Lebens, Frankfurt/M. 1941.

A. *Jungwirth,* Beziehung Schuberts zu Pölten, St. Pölten 1912.

W. *Kahl,* Verzeichnis des Schrifttums über Franz Schubert 1828–1928 (Kölner Beiträge zur Musikforschung 1), Regensburg 1938.

W. *Klatte,* Franz Schubert (Die Musik. Sammlung illustrierter Einzeldarstellungen 22 und 23), Leipzig n. d.

R. *Klein,* Schubertstätten, Wien 1972.

K. *Kobald,* Schubert und Schwind, Ein Wiener Biedermeierbuch, Zürich - Leipzig - Wien 1921.

_____ , Franz Schubert, Zürich - Leipzig - Wien 1921 (4th ed., 1948).

_____ , Der Meister des deutschen Liedes, Wien - Leipzig 1928.

H. *Költzsch,* Franz Schubert und seine Klaviersonaten (Sammlung musikwissenschaftlicher Einzeldarstellungen 7), Leipzig 1927.

A. *Kolb,* Franz Schubert. Sein Leben, Stockholm 1941.

H. *Kralik,* Schubert's Liederzyklen. „Die schöne Müllerin'', „Winterreise'' und „Schwanengesang'', Wien n. d.

F. *v. Kraus,* Beiträge zur Erforschung des malenden und poetisierenden Wesens in der Begleitung von Franz Schuberts Liedern, Mainz 1928 (2d ed.).

V. *Konen,* Schubert, Moskau 1959.

H. *Kreissle v. Hellborn,* Franz Schubert, Wien 1865.

G. R. *Kruse,* Franz Schubert, Bielefeld - Leipzig 1924.

C. *Lafite,* Das Schubertlied und seine Sänger, Wien 1928.

F. *Lange,* Franz Schubert und die Tanzmusik seiner Zeit, Wien 1906.

La Mara, Franz Schubert. Neu bearb. Einzeldruck aus den musikalischen Studienköpfen, Leipzig 1929.

P. *Landormy,* La vie de Schubert (Vies des hommes illustres 19), Paris 1928 (2d ed. 1942).

J. *Laufer,* Schubert, le Maitre du Romantisme et du Lyrisme en

musique, Paris 1961.

A. *Machát*, Schubert - Muzikant Bozć, Praha 1941.

H. *Markl*, Franz Schubert, Wien n. d.

T. L. *Meyer*, Franz Schubert. En Komponists Liv og Kunst, København 1946.

P. *Mies*, Schubert, der Meister des Liedes. Die Entwicklung von Form und Inhalt im Schubertschen Lied (M. Hesse's illustr. Handbücher 89), Berlin 1928.

_____ , Franz Schubert, Leipzig 1954.

J. *Müller-Blattau*, Franz Schuberts Leben und Werk, Königstein i. T. 1959.

A. *Nathansky*, Bauernfeld und Schubert, Wien 1906.

A. *Orel*, Der junge Schubert (Aus der Lehrzeit des Künstlers), Wien - Leipzig 1940.

H. *Osterheld*, Franz Schuberts Schicksal und Persönlichkeit, Stuttgart - Degerloch 1978.

E. *Pablé*, Das kleine Schubertbuch, Salzburg 1966.

B. *Paumgartner*, Die Schubertianer. Ein Beitrag zur Jahrhundertfeier, Wien 1928.

_____ , Franz Schubert, Zürich 1960.

R. *Petzoldt*, Franz Schubert. Sein Leben in Bildern, Leipzig 1955.

_____ , Franz Schubert. Leben und Werk, Leipzig n. d.

H. *v. d. Pforten*, Franz Schubert und das deutsche Lied, Leipzig 1916.

R. *Pitrou*, Franz Schubert. Vie intime, Paris 1928 (5th ed.).

J. C. *Prod'homme*, Schubert, raconté par ceux qui l'ont vu, Paris 1928.

J. *Reed*, Franz Schubert. The final Years, London 1972.

W. and P. *Rehberg*, Franz Schubert. Sein Leben und Werk, Zürich 1946.

A. *Reimann*, Franz Schubert. Sein Leben und seine Werke, Berlin 1873.

F. *Reininghaus*, Schubert und das Wirtshaus. Musik unter Metternich, Berlin 1979.

A. *Reissmann*, Franz Schubert. Sein Leben und seine Zeit, Berlin 1873.

R. *Rhein*, Schuberts Variationswerke (Diss.), Stuttgart 1960.

W. *Riezler*, Franz Schubert. Intrumentalmusik. Werkanalyse, Zürich 1967.

J. *Rissé*, Franz Schubert und seine Lieder, vol. 1 Müller-Lieder, vol. 2 Goethe-Lieder, Erfurt n. d.

E. *Roggeri,* Schubert. La vita. Le opere, Torino 1928.

A. *Schering,* Franz Schubert's Symphonie in H-Moll (Unvollendete) und ihr Geheimnis, Würzburg - Aumühle 1938.

H. G. *Schmidt,* Das Männerchorlied Franz Schuberts, Hildburghausen n. d.

E. *Schmitz,* Schuberts Auswirkung auf die deutsche Musik bis Hugo Wolf und Bruckner, Leipzig 1954.

E. *Schnapper,* Die Gesänge des jungen Schubert vor dem Durchbruch des romantischen Liedprinzips (Berner Veröffentlichungen zur Musikforschung 10), Bern - Leipzig 1937.

M. *Schneider,* Franz Schubert, Paris n. d.; German edition: Franz Schubert in Selbstzeugnissen und Bilddokumenten (Rowohlt-Monographien), Reinbek b. Hamburg 1958/1965.

M. and L. *Schochow* (ed.), Franz Schubert. Die Texte seiner einstimmig komponierten Lieder und ihre Dichter, Hildesheim - New York 1974.

K. *Schönewolf,* Franz Schubert, Ein grosser Volkskünstler, Berlin 1953.

G. *Schünemann,* Erinnerungen an Schubert. Joseph v. Spauns erste Lebensbeschreibung, Zürich 1936.

L. J. *Sedlitzky,* Beethoven und Schubert in Niederdonau, St. Pölten n. d.

A. *Silverstrelli,* Franz Schubert. Das wahre Gesicht seines Lebens, Salzburg - Leipzig 1939 (2d ed.).

P. *Simmer,* Franz Schubert, Wien 1947.

A. *Simon,* Die frühen Messen Schuberts, Karlsruhe 1968.

H. *Sittenberger,* Schubert, Zürich - Leipzig - Stuttgart 1928.

P. *Stefan,* Franz Schubert, Berlin 1928.

J. F. *Steffen,* Franz Schubert. Leben und Werk, Hamburg 1953.

R. *Stoeckl,* Die musikalische Gestaltung von Sprachform und Gehalt in Schuberts „Winterreise" (Diss.), Erlangen 1949.

W. *Tappert,* 70 Erlkönig-Kompositionen, Berlin 1906.

R. *Tenschert,* Du holde Kunst. Ein kleiner Schubert-Spiegel, Wien 1943.

H. J. *Therstappen,* Die Entwicklung der Form bei Schubert (Sammlung musikwissenschaftlicher Einzeldarstellungen 16), Leipzig 1931.

Y. *Tiénot*, Franz Schubert. Esquisse biographique, Paris - Bruxelles 1948.

A. *Trost*, Schuberts Bildnisse, Wien 1898.

E. *Valentin*, (ed.), Die schönsten Schubertbriefe, München - Wien 1975.

M. *Vancsa*, Schubert und seine Verleger, Wien 1905.

W. *Vetter*, Franz Schubert (Die grossen Meister der Musik), Potsdam 1934.

————— , Der Klassiker Schubert (2 vols.), Leipzig 1953.

H. *Wagemans*, Franz Schubert, Antwerpen 1952.

J. *Wechsberg*, Schubert. Sein Leben, Sein Werk. Seine Zeit. München, 1978 (Originally in English).

O. *Weigmann*, Schwinds Entwürfe für ein Schubertzimmer, München 1925.

F. *Weingartner*, Franz Schubert und sein Kreis (Schaubücher 24), Zürich -Leipzig 1929.

C. *Weingartner-Studer*, Franz Schubert. Sein Leben und Werk (Musiker-Reihe Basel 2), Olten 1947.

A. *Weinmann*, J. P. Gotthard als später Originalverleger Franz Schuberts (Wiener Archivstudien 2), Wien 1979.

A. *Weiss*, Franz Schubert, Wien 1928.

————— , Der Schubertsänger Johann Michael Vogl, Wien 1915.

R. *Werba*, Schubert und die Wiener. Der Volkstümliche Unbekannte, Wien 1978.

H. *Werlé*, Franz Schubert. Der Mensch und sein Werk, Bayreuth 1941.

————— , Franz Schubert in seinen Briefen und Aufzeichnungen, Leipzig 1948 (2d ed. 1955).

O. *Wheeler-S. Deucher*, Schubert und seine Freunde. Transl. into German by A. Kiszelényi, Würzburg - Wien 1955.

C. *Whitaker-Wilson*, Franz Schubert. Man and composer, London 1928.

R. *Wickenhauser*, Die Symphonien Franz Schuberts, Analytische Einführung (Erläuterungen zu Meisterwerken der Tonkunst 41) Leipzig n. d.

E. *Wilberforce*, Franz Schubert, A musical biography from the German of Dr. Heinrich Kreissle v. Hellborn, London 1866.

A. *Winkler*, Kaiser Franz und Franz Schubert, Wien 1929.

O. *Wissig*, Franz Schuberts Messen, Leipzig 1909.

E. *Ziese*, Schuberts Tod und Begräbnis in der ältesten

Darstellung, Grossdeuben n. d.

3. A few important articles

P. *Badura-Skoda,* Unbekannte Eigenschriften bekannter Schubertwerke in: Neue Zeitschrift für Musik 122 (1961), 502–506.

G. *Baum,* Schubert-Müllers Wintereise—neu gesehen, in: Neue Zeitschrift für Musik 128 (1967), 78–80.

O. *Biba,* Einige neue und wichtige Schubertiana im Archiv der Gesellschaft der Musikfreunde, in: Österreichische Musikzeitschrift 33 (1978), 604–610.

M. J. E. *Brown,* Schubert Derivatives in the Songs, in: Music & Letters 28 (1947), 207–213.

———, Schubert's Unfinished Symphony in D, in: Music & Letters 31 (1950), 101–109.

———, Recent Schubert Discoveries, in: Music & Letters 32 (1951), 349–361.

———, Some unpublished Schubert songs and song fragments, in: The Music Review 15 (1954), 93–102.

———, Schubert's two major Operas. A consideration of the possibility of actual stage production, in: The Music Review 20 (1959), 104–118.

———, Schubert: Discoveries of the Last Decade, in: The Musical Quarterly 57 (1971), 351–378.

F. *Burkhart,* Franz Schuberts „Deutsche Messe", in: Österreichische Musikzeitschrift 31 (1976), 565–573.

O. E. *Deutsch,* Schuberts Verleger, in: Der Bär, Leipzig 1928, 13–30.

———, Schuberts zwei Liederhefte für Goethe, in: Die Musik 21 (1928/29), 31–37.

———, Schuberts Popularität einst und jetzt, in: National-Zeitung, Basel, 1 July 1934.

———, Schuberts Aufnahme in England, in: Österreichische Musikzeitschrift 2 (1947), 21ff.

———, The Discovery of Schubert's Great C-Major Symphony. A Story in fifteen letters, in: The Musical Quarterly 38 (1952), 528ff.

———, The Schubert Catalogue: Corrections and Additions, in: Music & Letters 34 (1953), 25ff.

———, Schuberts „Ungarische Melodie" (D 817), in: Studia

musicologica, Tom 3 (1962), 89ff.

M. *Enzinger*, Franz von Bruchmann, der Freund J. Chr. Senns und des Grafen August v. Platen. Eine Selbstbiographie, in: Museum Ferdinandeum 10 (1930), 117–379.

C. *Floros*, Parallelen zwischen Schubert und Bruckner, in: Festschrift Othmar Wessely, Tutzing 1982, 133–145.

G. *Grove*, Schubert's great Symphony in C Nr. 10, in: The Musical Times 45 (1904), 523–528.

W. G. *Hill*, The Genesis of Schubert's posthumous Sonata in B flat major, in: The Music Review 12 (1951), 269–278.

E. *Hilmar*, Neue Funde, Daten und Dokumente zum symphonischen Werk Franz Schuberts, in: Österreichische Musikzeitschrift 33 (1978), 266–276.

R. *van Hoorickx*, Two Essays on Schubert, in: Revue Belge de Musicologie 24 (1970), 81–95.

E. *Laaf*, Schuberts grosse C-dur Symphonie. Erkennbare Grundlagen über Einheitlichkeit, in: Festschrift Friedrich Blume, Kassel 1963, 204–213.

Ch. *Landon*, Neue Schubert-Funde. Unbekannte Manuskripte im Archiv des Wiener Männergesang-Vereines, in: Österreichische Musikzeitschrift 26 (1969), 299–323.

Dies., Ein neuer Schubert-Brief, und einige Konsequenzen, in: Österreichische Musikzeitschrift 32 (1977), 545–554.

J. P. *Larsen*, zu Schuberts Vertonung des Liedes „Nur wer die Sehnsucht kennt", in: Gedenkschrift für Walther Vetter, Leipzig 1969, 277–281.

P. *Mies*, Die Entwürfe Franz Schuberts zu seinen letzten drei Klaviersonaten von 1828, in: Beiträge zur Musikwissenschaft 2 (1960), 52–68.

K. *Pfannhauser*, Zur Es-Dur Messe von Franz Schubert, in: Neue Zeitschrift f. Musik 119 (1958), 435.

F. *Racek*, Eine wiedergefundene Schuberthandschrift, in: Österreichische Musikzeitschrift 2 (1947), 18–20.

————, Von den Schubert-Handschriften der Stadtbibliothek, in: Festschrift zum hundertjährigen Bestehen der Wiener Stadtbibliothek (Wiener Schriften 4), Wien 1956, 98–124.

————, Franz Schuberts Singspiel „Der häusliche Krieg" und seine jetzt aufgefundene Ouverture, in: Biblos 12

(1963), 136–143.

J. *Reed,* How the "Great" C major was written, in: Music & Letters 56 (1975), 18–25.

H. *Truscott,* Schubert's String Quartet in G major, in: The Music Review 20 (1959), 119–145.

A. *Tyson,* Schubert and Terpsichore, in: The Musical Times 109 (1968), 812.

A. *Weinmann,* Eine österreichische Volkshymne von Franz Schubert, in: Österreichische Musikzeitschrift 27 (1972), 430–434.

———, Zwei neue Schubert-Funde, in: Österreichische Musikzeitschrift 27 (1972), 75–78.

R. *Werba,* Schubert und die Nachwelt, in: Österreichische Musikzeitschrift 33 (1978), 599–604.

O. *Wessely,* Franz Schuberts "Rastlose Liebe", ein neues Autograph, in: Musikerziehung 5 (1951/52), 208–213.

Index of Persons

(Not including the Chronology)

Ottenwald, Marie 29

Pachler, Marie Leopoldine 104
Paer, Ferdinando 47, 62, 74
Paganini, Niccoló 56
Palffy, Ferdinand v., Count 61, 62, 63, 65
Pamer, Michael 85, 86
Pennauer, Anton 41, 108
Pensel, Johann 86
Perigord, Dorothea, Duchess 24
Peters, Carl Friedrich 39
Pichler, Caroline 25, 26, 47, 91, 101, 128, 130
Pixis, Johann Peter 54
Pleyel, Ignaz 33
Preindl, Joseph 110
Probst, Heinrich 42, 43

Raimund, Ferdinand 72, 89, 98, 114
Reichardt, Johann Friedrich 81, 132
Reinöhl, Karl 132
Reischl, Florian 131
Ricordi, Giovanni 106
Ries, Ferdinand 48
Riotte, Philipp Jakob 66
Rochlitz, Johann Friedrich 15, 94, 109, 128, 134
Romberg, Andreas Jakob 48
Romberg, Bernhard 48, 55
Roner, Franziska v. Ehrenwerth (wife of Spaun)
Rosenbaum, Josef Karl 75
Roser, Franz 63, 66, 71
Rossi, Josef 128
Rossini, Gioacchino 42, 59, 64, 65, 66, 73, 76, 77, 79, 106, 131
Rozier (Rosier), Theodora 78
Ruess, Franz 55

Salieri, Antonio 14, 15, 59, 62
Salis-Seewis, Johann Gaudenz v. 97
Sauer, Ignaz 39
Sauer & Leidesdorf 40, 41
Scarlatti, Domenico 34
Scherer, Wilhelm 133

Schikaneder, Emanuel 61
Schiller, Friedrich v. 20, 75, 91, 92, 94, 95, 96, 106
Schindler, Anton 78
Schlag, Gerald 127
Schlechta, Franz Xaver 95
Schlegel, August Wilhelm 97
Schlegel, Friedrich 26, 91, 92, 95, 97, 98
Schneider, Hans 128
Schober, Franz v. 30, 39, 77, 95, 98, 99, 100, 101, 102, 110, 131, 133
Schoberlechner, Franz 50, 77
Scholz, Wenzel 73
Schönherr, Max 132
Schönstein, Karl v., Baron 78
Schott, Bernhard & Sons (publisher) 42, 130
Schreyvogel, Joseph 94
Schubert, Ferdinand 13, 14, 41
Schubert, Franz Theodor 13, 14
Schubert, Ignaz 103
Schunke, Karl 54
Schuppanzigh, Ignaz 27, 29, 56, 57
Schuster, Ignaz 71
Schwind, Moritz v. 9, 31, 83, 133
Scott, Walter 101
Scribe, Eugène 79
Sedlatzek, Johann 55
Sedlnitzky, Josef, Count 28
Seidl, Johann Gabriel 66, 131
Seidler, Herbert 90, 132, 133
Seipelt, Ignaz 50
Senefelder, Alois 34, 41, 130
Senn, Johann 21, 22
Seyfried, Ignaz 17, 51, 62, 66
Society of the Friends of Music see: Gesellschaft der Musikfreunde
Sonnleithner, Ignaz v. 27, 37, 105
Sonnleithner, Leopold v. 22, 37, 129
Sowinsky, Albert 86
Spaun, Josef v., Baronet 19, 28, 29, 31, 95, 99, 101, 133
Spina, Carl Anton 107
Spohr, Louis (Ludwig) 18, 48, 49, 79, 105
Spontini, Gasparo 17, 74
Stadler, Albert 95, 133